OUT OF THE ORDINARY

Anthea Dove i[illegible] commitment to justice [illegible] think of herself simply [illegible] rs in a Gloucestershire vi[illegible] [illegible]ical community of Hengrave Hall in Suffolk, she now lives in North Yorkshire. Together with her husband, she writes and does voluntary work, in addition to welcoming a large number of visitors. She has five children and five grandchildren.

Christina Caldwell is a professionally trained calligrapher. She lives in Stroud.

Out
OF THE
Ordinary

Calligraphy and Meditations

ANTHEA DOVE

Calligraphy by

CHRISTINA CALDWELL

First published 1994
Triangle
SPCK
Holy Trinity Church
Marylebone Road
London NW1 4DU

British Library Cataloguing in Publication Data
A catalogue record for this book is available from the British Library.
ISBN 0-281-04737-5

Typeset by Inforum, Rowlands Castle, Hants
Printed in Great Britain at
The University Press, Cambridge

For our dear mutual friends in Gloucestershire

Contents

Acknowledgements

Biblical quotations are taken from the following versions, as specified in the *Sources*, page 107.

Earth's
crammed
with heaven
and every
common bush

but only he
who sees
takes off his
shoes, the rest
sit round
it and pluck
blackberries

Preface

Earth's crammed with heaven
And every common bush afire with God:
But only he who sees takes off his shoes;
The rest sit round it, and pluck blackberries.
ELIZABETH BARRETT BROWNING

This book is written for ordinary people like myself. The fifty-two meditations are simple and short, thoughts that spring from the contemplation of the ordinary.

We do not become aware of the reality of God only in sunsets or on the mountain top; we encounter him daily in the stuff of our everyday lives. As Elizabeth Barrett Browning makes clear in her poem, we do not have to be Moses, we do not have to come across a burning bush. For 'every common bush is afire with God'.

These meditations are intended as springboards for the imagination, keys to open doors in the passages of the mind. They may lead us to think directly of God, of his people, of our world, of ourselves. In pondering on them, we can, like Brother Lawrence, practise the presence of God.

The book will be most helpful if the meditations are read slowly. Ideally it is not a book to read straight through. My hope is that through reading it people may find God in unexpected places and be led into a deeper relationship with him.

The meditations have been written in close co-operation with Christina Caldwell, the calligrapher. We are old friends, and though now living far apart we have both prayed and sought the inspiration of the Holy Spirit as this book has come into being.

Anthea Dove,
Whitby, 1994

Morning

New every morning is the love
Our waking and uprising prove.
JOHN KEBLE

I am one of those people who find it very hard to get out of bed. But once the brave act is accomplished, especially if I have managed it early, I am very glad to be up and enjoying the morning.

For me it is the best time of the day, the time when there is space to think and pray before the clutter of life starts crowding in: people, work, traffic, noise, things that must be done.

Early morning is a good time to meditate, to be still and alone before the Lord. It is also a good time to walk. In the country it is easier to be aware of the freshness of a new day, but in towns and cities too the air feels cleaner, the pavements are empty; we may even catch a glimpse of the sunrise.

In the morning we become aware of the potential of our day, a new day, which is a gift from God. We cannot know all that is going to happen, what new encounters we will make, how we will feel when that day is over. And in the morning, except for those who are overwhelmed by great sorrow, there is always a sense of a new beginning, of expectancy.

Gerard Manley Hopkins, in his poem 'God's Grandeur' where he laments the damage done to the world by human beings, sees morning as the sign of hope:

> And though the last lights off the black West went
> Oh, morning, at the brown brink eastward, springs—
> Because the Holy Ghost over the bent
> World broods with warm breast and with ah! bright wings.

Dear Lord, in the morning let me know your love.

And though the
last lights off
the black West went
oh morning,
at the brown brink
eastward, springs –
because the Holy Ghost
over the bent
world broods with
warm breast
and with, ah!
bright wings

Cup

Ordinary,
its round shape fits the hands,
the gnarled, ice-cold, shaking hands
that hold it—
a cup of hot tea
for a destitute old man.

A cup signifies generosity, both in giving and in receiving. Never, surely, was this exemplified better than in the actions of Christ on the night before his death.

> At supper with his friends, he took a cup of wine and when he had returned thanks he gave it to them. 'Drink all of you from this', he said. 'For this is my blood, the blood of the covenant, which is to be poured out for many for the forgiveness of sins.' (Matthew 26.27–28)

Christ used the cup for giving.

A few hours later, he knelt in prayer in the garden of Gethsemane, and cried out in great sadness and distress, 'My Father, if this cup cannot pass by without my drinking it, your will be done!' (Matthew 26.42)

This was the cup from which Christ received. To drink fully from that cup was to accept fully the dreadful suffering which was in store for him.

Both in giving the one cup and receiving from the other, he was expressing his great and generous love for us. He encourages us to begin to be generous too, when he says:

> 'If anyone gives a cup of water to one of these little ones, because he is a disciple, then in truth I tell you, he will most certainly not go without his reward'. (Matthew 10.42)

Over the centuries, most of us Christians have become doers and givers rather than receivers, active rather than passive. Occasionally, in rare moments of complete joy, we can identify with the writer of the twenty-third psalm and feel that our cup 'runneth over'. But in reflection we often become aware of our emptiness, and of a longing to be filled with God's love and God's power. When we hold ourselves still and in silence, we may indeed feel like a cup, empty but open to the outpouring of God's Spirit.

Alcuin, a theologian of the eighth century, prayed for the gifts of the Spirit.

> Give me, O Lord, I pray thee,
> firm faith, unwavering hope,
> perfect charity.
> Pour into my heart
> the spirit of wisdom and understanding,
> the spirit of counsel and ghostly strength,
> the spirit of knowledge and true godliness,
> and the spirit of thy holy fear.

Sun

I believe in the sun even when it is not shining.
I believe in love even when I cannot feel it.
I believe in God, even when he is silent.

I believe in the sun; in its power to revive our spirits. For days the skies have been grey, and yesterday it rained for hours. But this morning the sun is shining. The crocuses have opened their faces, the postman is whistling and everyone seems to be smiling.

The sun is surely the most powerful symbol of Jesus Christ. The sun gives light and warmth. It makes things grow. It brings life and happiness.

It is no wonder that in some religions of the world the sun itself was worshipped as a god. It was looked up to as the heroic conqueror of darkness in Ancient Egypt, Greece, Rome and among the Inca people of South America.

But the sun is a natural phenomenon, part of God's creation, and only a symbol of the Light of the World. It is Jesus who brings light in our darkness, who warms us with his compassion. It is his Spirit who comforts us in our weakness and sorrow, and helps us to grow in faith and love. Through his death and resurrection, Jesus has given us new life and filled us with Easter joy.

We may join with Erasmus, the Dutch scholar of the fifteenth century, in his prayer to 'The True Sun':

O thou, who art the true sun of the world,
ever rising, and never going down;
who by the most wholesome appearing and sight,
dost nourish and gladden all things in heaven
and earth;

we beseech thee mercifully to shine into our hearts,
that the night and darkness of sin, and the mists of error on every side,
being driven away by the brightness of thy shining within our hearts,
we may all our life walk without stumbling,
as in the daytime,
and being pure and clean from the works
of darkness,
may abound in all good works
which thou hast prepared for us to walk in. Amen.

Chain

A piece of chain
lying in the gutter.
Under the grime
it is silver.
I wonder who gave it,
who wore it,
who lost it.

To some extent, each of us is in chains. None of us is entirely free, and some of us are tightly bound by our heredity, our upbringing, our suffering, or our lovelessness.

A man or woman who has been cherished from birth, who has good health, a fine intellect, an attractive personality and plenty of money—such a one is more likely to have plenty of freedom.

The father of starving children feels he must steal and the unloved child is incapable of loving. They are not free to become fully the individuals God wants them to be, because of circumstances they cannot control.

It is sometimes difficult for people to accept this. They have little patience with those who try to discover why criminals behave as they do, and say that we should spend less time in trying to understand *why* people commit outrages and put all our efforts into curbing their activities.

Relatively speaking, it is not difficult for the comfortable to be virtuous, yet sadly so often they are the quickest to condemn others.

It is easy to forget that Jesus came on earth for sinners, that he chose to eat and drink with sinful people. There is only one fit to judge, and only one who knows the secrets of our hearts.

And just as it is only God who sees and knows us as we really are, it is only God who can set us free.

On July 12, 1739 Charles Wesley visited Newgate Prison in London. He wrote in his journal:

> I preached at Newgate to the condemned felons and visited one of them in his cell, sick of a fever, a poor black that had robbed his master. I told him of One who came down from heaven to save lost sinners and him in particular: described the sufferings of the Son of God. . . . He listened with all the signs of eager astonishment; the tears trickled down his cheeks while he cried, What! was it for me? Did God suffer all this for so poor a creature as me?
> I left him waiting for salvation.

Inspired by this experience, Charles Wesley wrote his hymn 'And can it be . . .?'

> Long my imprisoned spirit lay
> Fast bound in sin and nature's night
> Thine eye diffused a quickening ray—
> I woke, the dungeon flamed with light,
> My chains fell off, my heart was free
> I rose, went forth, and followed thee.

Lord, help me not to judge or condemn others,
but only to see them as you see them,
and so seeing, to love them.

Bread

Bread,
newly baked,
warm and smelling wonderful,
made from wheat,
blessed by the sun,
blessed by the rain,
work of human hands.

Bread is for sharing.

Though we are many,
we are one body
because we all share
in one bread.
(Anglican Eucharist)

When Jesus fed the five thousand it was with bread miraculously shared. It may have been miraculous because of his divine power, or because all those people were inspired to share from their own resources.

He shared bread, too, at supper on the night before he died, choosing something so simple and basic to our needs as a symbol of himself. He broke the bread and gave it to his disciples, with significance for all people and for all time. The eucharistic bread is not only Jesus giving himself to us for personal benefit. It is Jesus giving himself to us so that we may share his light and his goodness with all those we meet.

And although the Eucharist is central to the faith of a good number of Christians it is not the only means of celebrating God's love in the sharing of bread. For those ordinary Christians of different traditions who long to be united as one church, one people, the Eucharist is a stumbling-block. There is shame and sadness at those services where some worshippers are excluded from the sacrament. For this reason many people choose instead to gather at an agape or love-feast where they can all share bread as a symbol of Christ.

An Irish friend of mine visited a shanty town outside Santiago in Chile, and was invited to share a meal in one of the 'houses'—a shack made from cardboard and corrugated iron. To his surprise, for he had found them to be a brave and smiling people in spite of their circumstances, he discovered when he arrived that the family was dejected and shamefaced. One of the sons, looking crestfallen, held a plastic bottle containing a fizzy drink that had long since gone flat. The father said in a low voice, 'I am sorry. There is nothing to eat.' There were tears in the mother's eyes.

Then suddenly a hand pushed through a hole in the wall of the hut, a hand holding half a loaf of bread. The mother took it and the hand withdrew. Now the family were all smiles. They sat on the mud floor and shared the stale bread and the 'wine' with my friend. It was a celebration, a thanksgiving and a sharing of love, made possible through the generous act of a neighbour.

> Lord, give us this day our daily bread.
> Show us the way to share our bread with the hungry,
> and the Bread of Life
> with all who long to share in the Eucharist together.

Garden

One is nearer God's Heart in a garden
Than anywhere else on earth.
DOROTHY GURNEY

I walk in my garden not so much seeking peace as assured of it. I have only to step from my door to the small patch of earth where flowers grow to become a different person. My small worries vanish and even the great burdens seem lighter.

Walking in the garden is like praying. My mind is still, my senses sharpened, and the gentle presence is there; near, above, around me.

The seventeenth-century poet Andrew Marvell describes what happens to him in a garden:

Meanwhile the mind from pleasure less
Withdraws into its happiness . . .

Annihilating all that's made
To a green thought in a green shade.

But for me it is hardly a thought. My mental powers are at rest. In wonder I gaze at the lilies, I breathe in the scent of the roses. I watch the tiny ladybird, and listen to the bee's hum. I do no work in the garden. I do not know the names of many of the plants. It is enough, more than enough, just to be there and marvel.

Sometimes the promise in Jeremiah comes into my mind:

Their soul will be like a watered garden.
They will sorrow no more.
(Jeremiah 31.12)

Lord, grant everyone access to a garden.

Needle

a time
for sewing
(Ecclesiastes 3.7)

I have trouble in threading a needle; still more in using it. In other words, I am no good at sewing. True, I am a degree better than one of my daughters, who turns up the hems of her skirts with a stapler. I can at least sew on a button.

But I wish I could sew well, and make my own clothes. When I read about 'the perfect wife' at the end of the Book of Proverbs, I am torn between shame and envy:

> A perfect wife—who can find her?
> She is far beyond the price of pearls.
>
> . . .
>
> She is always busy with wool and with flax,
> she does her work with eager hands.
>
> . . .
>
> She sets her hands to the distaff,
> her fingers grasp the spindle.
>
> . . .
>
> She makes her own quilts,
> she is dressed in fine linen and purple.
> (Proverbs, 31.10, 13, 19, 22)

The lady in question had many other talents besides those listed in this excerpt. 'No bread of idleness for her' is an unsurprising later comment.

I wish I could be like her, good with my hands, good at sewing, knitting, dressmaking, embroidery. I wish I could play an instrument. I wish I could paint and draw . . . and suddenly I see how silly I am. I come to my senses and remember that there are a variety of gifts and I do have a share in some of them.

Every one of us is gifted by God in some way. Let us rejoice in our gifts and use them to the best of our ability rather than waste time wishing for other talents. I can't sew, but I can read. I can't knit but I can walk. I can't embroider but I can cook.

The Lord has blessed me in so many ways; I want to sing my thankfulness to him:

> My soul, give thanks to the Lord.
> All my being, bless his holy name.
> My soul, give thanks to the Lord
> and never forget all his blessings.
> (Psalm 103.1–2)

Children

Heaven lies about us
in our infancy.
WORDSWORTH

Seeing the little girl running barelegged through the grass in the sunshine, I was suddenly transported back to my own childhood, to the time of unclouded skies and endless summers.

And then I remembered that it was not really like that. I remembered that I was vulnerable and afraid and struggling to please, but because I was too young to be any other way, I was incapable of deceit.

In St John's Gospel we are told that when Jesus saw Nathaniel coming towards him, he said, 'There truly is an Israelite in whom there is no deception' (John 1.47). Nathaniel must have been almost unique in the world's history! From a very young age we learn not to show our true feelings, to pretend to be other than we are. By the time most of us are grown up, out 'real' self is well concealed, not only from strangers but even from those who know and love us.

HEAVEN LIES ABOUT US
in our infancy

Yet hidden away inside us is the same little girl or boy who played in the sunshine, who had not yet learnt to pretend. Even if it were possible, would it be wise to try to recapture that innocence and openness?

I believe it is a risk worth taking. It is only when our defences are down that we can relate to one another in truth, that we can become people of integrity.

Jesus said, 'I tell you solemnly, unless you change and become like little children, you will never enter the kingdom of heaven'. (Matthew 18.3)

Lord, give us the courage we need to reveal our true selves to others.
Let us not be afraid to take this risk in love
and become as little children for your sake.

Bed

On my bed I remember you.
(Psalm 63.6)

The writer of Psalm 63 prays on his bed. My bed, too, is a place for praying, for loving, for resting, for dreaming. My bed is warm, my mattress firm, my sheets clean.

Sleep is a blessing. At the end of a stressful day I collapse wearily, gratefully on my bed, relaxing in the comfort of that private place, glad of the stillness, the familiarity, looking forward to my dreams.

It is not a case of making my bed and lying on it. I deserve to rest easy at night no more than those in my town who have to sleep in bus shelters or cardboard boxes.

I remember that Jesus himself was homeless. He said,

> Foxes have holes
> and the birds of the air have nests,
> but the Son of Man has nowhere to lay his head.
> (Matthew 8.20)

In our town we have a hostel for the homeless. We have a lot of people interested and trying to help. But it is not enough, the hostel is full. However cold the night, some people have to go without a bed, without a roof over their heads, and sadly it is often the ones most in need.

> Lord, you know me.
> You know that I live in comfort
> and sleep well every night.
> You also know that I am aware
> of those who have no shelter from the cold,
> no place they can call home.
> Show me what I should do.

FOXES
HAVE
HOLES
& THE
BIRDS
OF THE
AIR HAVE
NESTS

SEEK LOVE
IN THE PITY OF
ANOTHER'S WOE
IN THE GENTLE
RELIEF OF
ANOTHER'S CARE
IN THE DARK-
NESS OF NIGHT
AND THE
WINTER'S SNOW
IN THE NAKED
AND OUTCAST
SEEK LOVE
THERE

WILLIAM BLAKE

Dead Bird

Why do I grieve
over a dead bird,
when the whole world
is weighed down
by human suffering?

It lay in the path outside the front door, a very young bird, dead.

Seeing it had fallen to the ground, I felt an immediate rush of anger towards God. For did not Jesus say, specifically: 'Not one (sparrow) falls to the ground without your Father knowing'? (Matthew 10.29).

But then I thought about it and understood. Jesus did not promise that God would save the sparrow, only that he knew about the fall.

And so it is with us. God does not feed the hungry in the desert, or rescue children from a burning house, or save the young mother dying of cancer. But he knows.

Perhaps God is not all-powerful. Perhaps there are other mysterious reasons why he does not intervene in human suffering. But he *is* all-loving. When the sparrow falls, the innocent are tortured, the despairing are driven to suicide, he is there. He is Love itself, and when we feel compassion for another's sorrow, we will find him.

> Seek Love in the pity of another's woe,
> In the gentle relief of another's care.
> In the darkness of night and the winter's snow
> In the naked and outcast—seek love there.
>
> WILLIAM BLAKE

Lord, you promised to be with us always,
even to the end of time.
In times of distress,
let us be aware of your presence.

Weed

What is a weed?
A plant whose virtues
have not been discovered.
RALPH WALDO EMERSON

I see a little plant growing in a crack in the path. I bend down and tug it out in one ruthless movement. I am about to toss it on to a pile of garden rubbish when I happen to glance down at the plant. Something about it catches my eye. I stop and begin to examine it. I see that it is delicate and beautiful.

And so I ask, 'Is this a weed? Who decides what is a weed and what is a flower, what must be cherished and what thrown away?' I am not a botanist, not even a gardener, and I do not know the answers to these questions.

Recently I listened to a sermon on one of the parables of Jesus: the story of the tares—weeds—sown among the wheat. When his disciples asked Jesus to explain the parable, he said,

> The field is the world; the good seed are the children of the kingdom; but the tares are the children of the wicked one. (Matthew 13.38 AV).

The preacher told us that there are evil men and women among us today. He cited as an example those who go out to developing countries to teach people about birth control.

I was uncomfortable with this homily. It seemed equally arguable that the evil ones could be those who try to prevent the teaching of methods of birth control in countries where so many children die of starvation. And I wondered by what authority the preacher made his judgements.

The abortion issue also came to mind. Both those who want to stop abortion and those who believe it is a woman's right to choose whether to terminate her pregnancy feel passionately that they are not only right but are acting from humane motivation. The extremists on either side view the others as evil.

I conclude that God alone can sort out the tares from the wheat. Of course we have a right and a duty to campaign for those things we believe in, but we do not have a right to judge the motives of others, or condemn them.

As for my weed, I have planted it next to the roses. I hope it will grow again.

> Love does not rejoice at wrongdoing, but finds its joy in the truth. It is always ready to make allowances, to trust, to hope and to endure whatever comes. (1 Corinthians 13.6–7)

Lord, let me not judge others,
and especially, let me not condemn them.

Daisy

The most ordinary flower,
unnoticed, trodden underfoot,
but still, a flower,
symbol of life and beauty,
God's creation.

Looking at a flower—whether it is a common daisy in the grass, a rare orchid blooming in a hothouse, the first brave snowdrop brightening the dark earth, or a tiny violet hidden in a hedgerow—I am moved to adore my God who made all things bright and beautiful.

Jesus looked at flowers, the lilies of the field, and saw their loveliness. He said, 'I say unto you that Solomon in all his glory was not arrayed like one of these' (Luke 12.27).

When we look at a flower, we see perfection, we see a miracle, that which God has made, that which reflects his glory. We experience a lifting of the heart, in praise and adoration. If we go on looking long enough, we begin to see that the flower is, as we are ourselves, an expression of life itself, of all things that grow and flourish on our planet.

And then, our eyes still on the daisy in the grass, we may be caught up in the conviction that the whole of Nature is somehow united in response to God's generosity, that there is a silent song of praise rising in glad worship through all creation.

An Englishwoman, contemplating a daisy, imagines the whole earth singing. Her Caribbean sister looks at a more exotic flower and prays:

> Halleliuh, Lord!
> All green tings an hibiscus praises Lord.
>
> GRACE NICHOLS

Are these women fanciful? Or are they justified in following the precedent of the three young men who sang from the heart of the fiery furnace:

> O let the earth bless the Lord
> To him be highest glory and praise for ever.
> And you, mountains and hills, O bless the Lord.
> And you, all plants of the earth, O bless the Lord.
> And you, fountains and springs, O bless the Lord.
> To him be highest glory and praise for ever.
> And you, rivers and seas, O bless the Lord.
> And you, creatures of the sea, O bless the Lord.
> And you, every bird in the sky, O bless the Lord.
> And you, wild beasts and tame, O bless the Lord.
> To him be highest glory and praise for ever.
> And you, children of men, O bless the Lord.
> To him be highest glory and praise for ever.
>
> (Daniel 3.74–82)

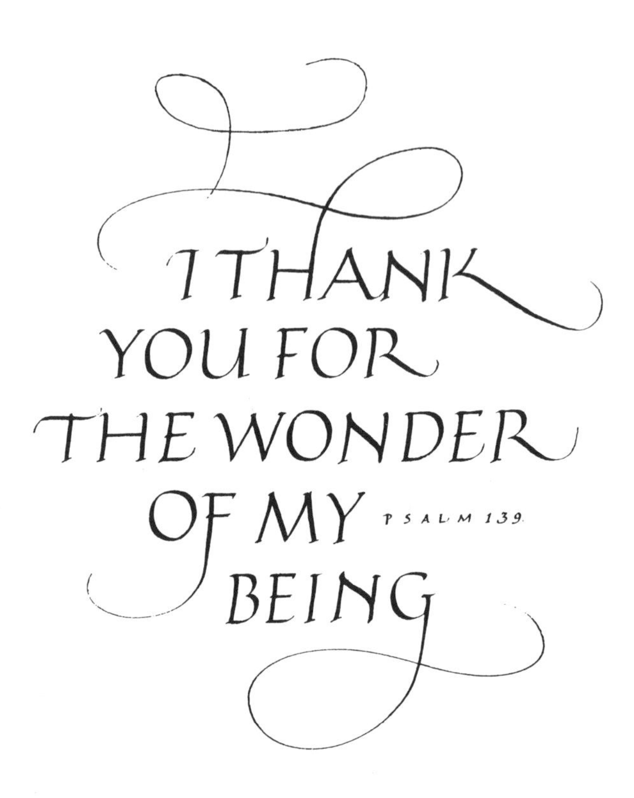

Dust

It catches my eye, the layer of it on the mantelpiece. I frown, ashamed. Then I smile, seeing it is the brightness of the sunshine which has revealed the dust to me, as God in his all-forgiving love sometimes makes plain our sinfulness.

It is a chastening experience for some of us to go to church on Ash Wednesday and stand before the priest who marks our foreheads with a sombre cross of ashes and says, 'Remember, man, that you are dust and to dust you will return.'

I find that for once I do not even resent being addressed as 'man'. It seems inappropriate to be concerned about sexism when faced with the awful reality of my nothingness. For in relation to God we are puny ephemeral creatures.

And yet there is a paradox.

Reading Psalm 139, I can say with sincerity, 'I thank you for the wonder of my being.' We who are dust, are also wonderful, made in the likeness of God himself, gifted and blessed with intelligence and feeling, with bodies, minds and souls and the capacity for delight and joy, hope and love.

To understand this paradox—that we can be insignificant and marvellous at the same time, we need to grow in the virtue of humility. It is not easy to be truly humble and a lot of the time we 'get it wrong'.

So many of us make a habit of putting ourselves down. Someone says, 'Your hair is beautiful' and we respond, 'It needs washing.' Some people have a genuine sense of their own worthlessness and are quite unable to accept themselves as lovable. Others enjoy an unthinking self-satisfaction, blind to their own complacency.

Perhaps our best chance of achieving true humility is to make time to reflect in quietness on our own attitudes and pray to God to grace us with this gift.

In this prayer, John Donne shows his awareness of the danger and wrong of placing too little value on ourselves:

> Eternal and most glorious God,
> who hast stamped the soul of man with thine Image,
> received it into thy Revenue,
> and made it a part of thy Treasure;
> Suffer us not so to undervalue ourselves,
> nay, so to impoverish thee
> as to give away these souls for nothing
> and all the world is nothing
> if the soul must be given for it.
> Do this, O God,
> for his sake who knows our natural infirmities,
> for he had them,
> and knows the weight of our sins,
> for he paid a dear price for them,
> thy Son, our Saviour Jesus Christ. Amen.
>
> JOHN DONNE

Crumb

Crumb on the carpet
sign of a careless housewife.
Crumb, sign of broken bread.

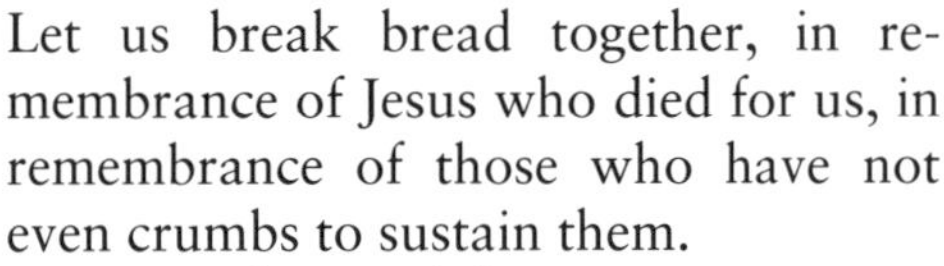

Let us break bread together, in remembrance of Jesus who died for us, in remembrance of those who have not even crumbs to sustain them.

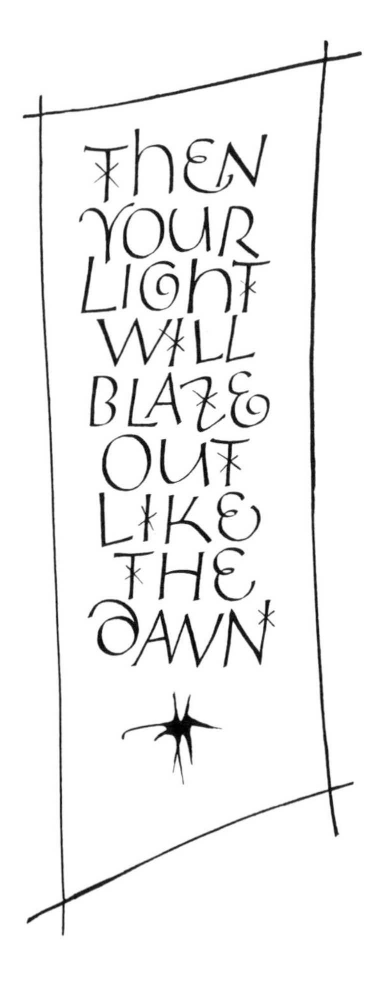

A crumb is a leftover scrap, something not needed by those who have plenty. In the story of Dives and Lazarus, the rich man did not even realize that the poor man at his gate was longing for the crumbs that fell from his food-laden table.

We have no such excuse. We do know that our brothers and sisters in the developing countries are hungry. We do know that we eat too much.

Christopher Smart, the eighteenth-century poet, wrote:

> For charity is cold
>   in the multitude of possessions,
> and the rich are covetous
>   of their crumbs.
>
> CHRISTOPHER SMART

This was a sad indictment of the rich. In global terms, almost every inhabitant of the first world in our day is rich, and many of us are covetous of our crumbs. In other words, we hold on not only to what we need and what we enjoy, but to things which are superfluous to our needs and enjoyments.

Thousands of years ago, the Old Testament prophets were urging the people of God to feed the hungry. In Isaiah we read of the sort of fast that pleases God:

> Is it not sharing your bread with the hungry and
> sheltering the homeless poor;
> if you see someone lacking clothes, to clothe him,
> and not to turn away from your own kin?
> Then your light will blaze out like the dawn
> And your wound be quickly healed over.
>
> (Isaiah 58.7–8)

Of course it is not a simple thing to share the world's goods; the politics and economics are too much for most of us to grasp. Individually, too, it is not easy to decide how much to give or what particular cause to support.

But most of us can give more than crumbs. Most of us can live more simply.

Lord, help us to listen when the poor are crying.
Let us be cheerful givers,
willing to share and willing to work for justice in our world.

Cream

'With cream?'
asks the waitress
with a speculative smile.
I weaken.
'Yes, please' I say.

The nursery rhyme paints a charming picture:

> Curlilocks, Curlilocks wilt thou be mine?
> Thou shalt not wash dishes nor yet feed the swine,
> But sit on a cushion and sew a fine seam
> And feed upon strawberries, sugar and cream.

Cream is a symbol of excess, delicious excess. As the advertisements tell us, it is 'naughty but nice'.

Followers of Jesus, living two thousand years after his birth, know they are called to live simply, to shun materialism and greed. Not for us a life of luxury, of champagne and caviar, of diamonds, fur coats, and Rolls Royces. It is our vocation, after all, not only to side with, but to identify with the poor.

And yet . . .? Surely there are moments in our lives when a little self-indulgence does no harm, but is positively good for us?

The creator of all things made strawberries, sugar, and cream for our enjoyment. The Son of God was delighted when Mary poured a jar of very costly ointment over his head. He spent his ministry in fasting, praying, and teaching, but sometimes he also went to parties.

There is a time in all our lives for practising restraint and austerity, perhaps especially in Advent and Lent as preparation for the great Christian feasts of the Incarnation and the Resurrection.

But most of us also need time to let go and have fun, to take pleasure in the good things of life: Nature, music, sex, sport, or whatever we enjoy and is appropriate for us.

Cream represents that which is delightfully excessive—'over the top' as we say nowadays—intemperate. In something of the same sense, the metaphysical poet George Herbert chooses cream as a strange metaphor to express his fervent, overflowing love for God.

King of Glory, King of Peace,
I will love thee;
And that love may never cease,
I will move thee.

Thou hast granted my request,
Thou hast heard me;
Thou didst note my working breast,
Thou hast spared me.

Wherefore with my utmost art
I will sing thee,
And the cream of all my heart
I will bring thee.

Lord, help me to be the person you want me to be,
living according to your hopes and desires,
with the wisdom to know when to fast and when to feast.

Dog

A dog may be
Man's best friend,
but he is not usually
the postman's!

In the Gospel of Matthew, Jesus encounters a Canaanite woman. At first he refuses to heal her daughter, saying he was sent only 'to the lost sheep of the House of Israel'. He goes on to compare the woman and her nation to house-dogs.

'Lord,' she said 'help me.' He replied, 'It is not fair to take the children's food and throw it to the house-dogs'. She retorted, 'Ah yes, sir; but even the house-dogs can eat the scraps that fall from their master's table'. Then Jesus answered her, 'Woman, you have great faith. Let your wish be granted.' And from that moment her daughter was well again. (Matthew 15.25–28).

This is one of those passages which puzzle and even dismay people. Jesus, whom we know to be all-compassionate, seems on the face of it to be hard and intolerant.

Matthew
15

Lord, she said, help me.
he replied, It is not fair
to take the children's
food and throw it to the
house-dogs. She retorted,
Sir, even the house-dogs
can eat the scraps that
fall from the master's
table. Then Jesus said,
Woman, you have great
faith, let your wish be
granted. And from
that moment her
daughter was made well.

Some people have tried to explain this by suggesting that Jesus was teasing the woman. This seems unlikely because she was in no fit state to be teased, frantic as she was for her daughter to be healed.

Others, studying the life of Jesus, believe that he went on learning and maturing as a human being throughout his life. Luke's Gospel tells us that, under the care of Mary and Joseph, he 'increased in wisdom and in stature' (Luke 2.52)—surely an implication that he was not born perfectly wise.

We know that Jesus was like us in all things but sin. He was a human being, a man of his time and place brought up with the biases of his own people. He needed to grow, and the Canaanite woman helped him. Remarkably she succeeded in changing the attitude of Jesus and in freeing him from the prejudice we call racism.

But if Jesus was a racist, then surely he was a sinner? I think not. To be prejudiced in any way through the conditioning of our upbringing and environment is not in itself evil. We are wrong if we close our minds, refusing to be open to the greater wisdom of others. We are wrong if we deliberately use our prejudices to hurt. But Jesus did neither of these things. He allowed the Canaanite woman to change him.

Jesus the man was not carved out of stone, changeless and perfect from the word go. He was human: he grew and learnt and changed and matured. One of his teachers was another human being, the one who in Matthew's gospel was likened to a dog.

To say such things about Jesus is not in any way to belittle his stature, or to question his divinity. Rather it is to love and revere him even more, because as a human being he took on not only our flesh but our weakness, and still became the way, the truth and the life.

Lord Jesus,
the very thought of what you have done
fills us with wonder, love and praise.
We thank you for your humanity in sharing our lives,
and your divinity in redeeming us.

Home

There's no place
like home.
J.H. PAYNE

I would like to feel that my house is a place where God is to be found.

But I have to ask: where *is* he to be found? *Where* is his dwelling-place? God is everywhere. God is closer to us than our breath. God is in heaven, wherever that may be. He is present in the Eucharist, and some people believe that he is present in the tabernacles of their churches. The holy, consecrated bread which has become Jesus, is reserved as a sacrament, so people genuflect in reverence before the tabernacle.

I believe that it is true that the presence of God is more powerfully felt in some places than others, especially places where people have been praying for centuries. It is also true that his presence is more profoundly felt among some people than among others, notably among those who, through their wholehearted response to the Holy Spirit and by their steadfast witness to the truth, have become transparent in their goodness and simplicity.

There seems little reason for trying to pinpoint where God is to be found, since it is a mystery beyond our understanding. Let us be content, with the writer of Psalm 84, to long to be in God's presence:

> How lovely is your dwelling place,
> Lord, God of hosts.
> My soul is longing and yearning,
> is yearning for the courts of the Lord.
> My heart and my soul ring out their joy
> to God, the living God.

. . .

They are happy, who dwell in your house,
for ever singing your praise.
(Psalm 84.2, 3, 5)

For me the most overwhelming thought about God's dwelling is the promise Jesus made:

If anyone loves me he will keep my word,
and my Father will love him,
and we shall come to him
and make our home with him.
(John 14.23)

Dear Lord, I pray that you will make your home with me.

Ring

With this ring
I thee wed,
with my body
I thee worship,
and with all my worldly goods
I thee endow.

Solemnization of Marriage,
The Book of Common Prayer.

I look at the ring on the third finger of my left hand. The gold has worn thinner over the long years. Thinking of my marriage, I feel profoundly thankful to God and to my husband. On our anniversary, friends will congratulate us on staying together 'for better, for worse, in sickness and in health'.

But I think of those of my children who do not want to marry, and of my friends who are divorced. Marriage was once the norm in western society, and arguably it is still the ideal, but I am fearful of complacency on the part of us, the lucky ones.

It is true that our marriage was a sacrament, that we have put effort into making it work, that we have struggled through difficult times, that we pray together. But I think it is also true that we are lucky, lucky to have succeeded where others, equally loving, equally committed, have failed—failed, that is, in the particular relationship of marriage.

In the second half of this century there has been a gradual shift in attitudes towards sex and marriage. Many people no longer see the family as the basis of society and they value freedom above security and stability.

Most young people are not practising Christians and they would choose to be married in church only for the romantic tradition. The alternative of a registry office has the attraction of simplicity but some of those who want to make a commitment to each other feel this too is unnecessary. They ask: 'What difference will a piece of paper make?'

Still others look around them and see that half the marriages in our society now end in divorce. They begin to question. They want to be honest with each other, and although their love may be strong and true, they know that people often fall out of love, or become attracted to someone else, or simply grow away from each other. They value their independence, their careers, their fulfilment. They feel unable to make a lifelong commitment, and so they decide not to marry.

This is not the Christian way, but increasingly it is the way young people think and act. It seems right that those of us who married in church and have stayed married should respect their honesty and desire for freedom. God will not judge us on whether or not we are wearing a wedding ring.

A prayer for all lovers:

> Almighty Father,
> you have created all mankind
> to glorify you in body and in spirit.
> Give these your children joy in one another,
> as living temples of the Holy Spirit,
> and bring them by this joy to know and share
> in your creative and redeeming love.
> (Marriage Service, *The Alternative Service Book*)

Flame

Come, Holy Spirit,
fill the hearts of your faithful
and enkindle in them the fire of your love.

When I pray, I listen to God the Father. I think of Jesus. But for some reason I 'neglect' the Holy Spirit, the one who dwells within me, ready to comfort and inspire me.

When I look at the bright flame in the heart of my fire, I am reminded of the flames that appeared on the heads of the disciples at Pentecost. I realize that my own response to the warmth and light of the Spirit within me is poor and weak.

These lines are recited in some churches on Pentecost Sunday:

Come, thou Father of the poor,
Come with treasures which endure,
Come thou light of all that lives!

. . .

Heal our wounds, our strength renew
On our dryness pour thy dew
Wash the stains of guilt away.
Bend the stubborn heart and will
Melt the frozen, warm the chill;
Guide the steps that go astray.

Attributed to ARCHBISHOP LANGTON

I am aware of my own dryness, my own chill. I need the flame to be fanned within me.

There is a story of a Desert Father who was approached by a disciple. The young man said that he had done all in his power to fast and pray and obey every rule. He asked what more he could do. The teacher simply said, 'Be a living flame.'

It is not enough to 'be good', and to stick to the rules. If we want to live as brothers and sisters of Jesus Christ, we need to be open to the Holy Spirit, to allow him to possess our souls so that we may burn brightly as living witnesses to his love.

Come Holy Ghost, Creator, come
From thy bright heavenly throne.
Come take possession of our souls
And make them all thy own.

. . .

O guide our minds with thy blest light
With love our hearts inflame,
And with thy strength which ne'er decays
Confirm our mortal frame.

Attributed to RABANUS MAURUS

Bible

> *Bible,*
> *bestseller.*
> *Who reads it?*

Much of our faith is based on Scripture. Jews, Christians and many seekers after truth read it, study it and hold it in reverence: the holy book. Those banished to the BBC's Desert Island are allowed to have a copy! The Bible is one thing that those Christians of different traditions who struggle so hard for unity have in common.

People use it differently: as literature, as history, as a curiosity, as the Word of God. Some people continue to take literally every word of Scripture, in face of all its contradictions. Scholars and theologians study the Bible in great detail, while others, like the first Queen Elizabeth, find solace through reading it:

> I walke manie times . . . into the pleasant fieldes of the Holye Scriptures, where I pluck up the goodlie greene herbes of sentences, eate them by reading, chewe them up musing, and laie them up at length in the seat of memories . . . so I may the lesse perceive the bitterness of this miserable life.
>
> QUEEN ELIZABETH I

Scripture can be inspiring to us in our daily lives. When we listen attentively, with open minds and hearts, even to the most familiar passages, we are often, if not invariably, struck as though by some personal message from God. This morning, for me, it was two lines from Psalm 143:

In the morning let me know your love
for I put my trust in you.
(Psalm 143.8)

Having wakened with some anxiety, I found reassurance in these words.

The Bible is a comprehensive treasury. If we read it from beginning to end, we may enjoy its wonderful stories like those of Ruth, or Philip and the Ethiopian eunuch; we may shudder at the way the Jews of the Old Testament sometimes saw God as being so full of cruel vengeance; we may delight in the poetry of Isaiah and the Song of Solomon, and identify with the human emotions of those who wrote the psalms. Above all, we will learn, especially through the life of Christ, to know the love and mercy of our God.

In the eighth century, the Northumbrian monk, Bede, wrote this prayer, appropriate for all of us who have been blessed by the reading of Scripture:

And I pray Thee, merciful Jesus,
that as Thou has graciously granted me
to drink down sweetly from the Word
which tells of Thee,
so wilt Thou kindly grant
that I may come at length to Thee,
the fount of all wisdom,
to stand before Thy face for ever.

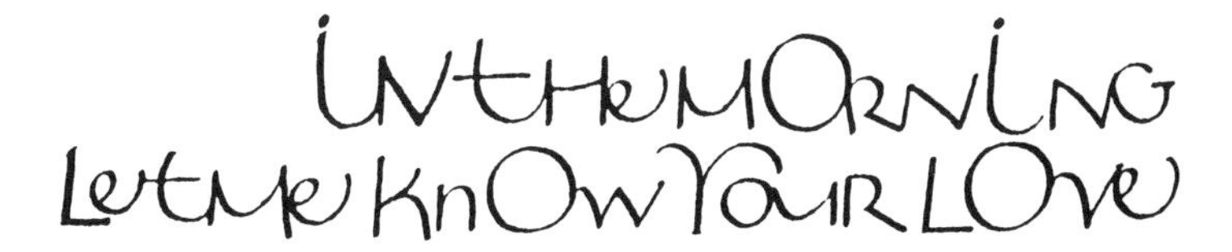

Moth

Can a moth ever be more beautiful
than a butterfly?
It is said that gentlemen prefer blondes,
but sometimes the quiet ones,
the muted browns and greys
draw us by their understated loveliness.

In the book of Genesis we read the story of Rachel and Leah. Leah was the moth to Rachel's butterfly. 'There was no sparkle in Leah's eyes, but Rachel was shapely and beautiful.' (Genesis 29.17)

Jacob loved Rachel, but both sisters loved him. Their father, Laban, promised Jacob that if he worked for seven years he would be given Rachel as his bride. But when the time was up, he sent Leah under cover of darkness to sleep with Jacob in his tent. In the morning, when Jacob discovered the trick that had been played on him, he was very angry. We can imagine the humiliation of Leah.

It is hard to be the not-so-attractive sister, the also-ran, second-best. The majority of us are Leahs rather than Rachels. Probably there has never been so much emphasis on the importance of good looks as there is at the present time. Day by day the advertisements on television encourage us to want to be beautiful; superficially beautiful that is, not in the sense that mother Teresa of Calcutta is beautiful.

There is some good advice to read in Peter's first letter, where he says:

> 'Do not dress up for show: doing up your hair, wearing gold bracelets and fine clothes; all this should be inside, in a person's heart, imperishable: the ornament of a sweet and gentle disposition—that is what is precious in the sight of God.' (1 Peter 3.3)

This makes uplifting reading, but perhaps we may be forgiven if we believe it is also pleasing to God—not to mention those we meet—when we make the best of our appearance.

The world of Nature is beautiful, and gives us pleasure. We too can please the eyes of those we meet by taking care of how we look. Greasy hair, dirty hands and slovenly dress may be trivial in the scheme of things, but they please no one.

The moth is not showy, but pleasant to look upon and on closer examination, beautiful.

Lord, help us to have a sensible and cheerful attitude towards
our appearance,
and to be confident in your love and in our own worth.

Walking-stick

Sturdy,
made of ash,
rough to look at,
smooth to hold:
Luke's father's
father's father's
walking stick.

My walking-stick evokes memories. There is no need to go anywhere. It is enough to sit still, holding it and remembering so many days of brimming pleasure.

Today I think of one such day, one such walk, along the east coast of England from Hayburn Wyke southwards. It was the beginning of July, before the summer gets tired. There were a few clouds, but the sky was blue and far, and sheer below it the sea was a deeper blue and almost calm. Not so the great fields of barley on our right, tossed into wild waves by the fresh south wind, another kind of ocean, pale green and limitless to the horizon. On our left, at the very edge of the cliff, small bright flowers brightened the path. There were no other people, no buildings in sight. The only sounds were the whispering of the wind in the barley, the murmur of the tide below us and a skylark high above. On walks such as this I feel like Enoch, who walked with God. For in the unbelievable beauty of Nature it is easy to believe in God and to be aware of his presence.

So I hold the walking-stick in my hands and remember. Yes, I know that it is vital to live in the present moment (given that the present moment is bearable), that it is foolish to make too many plans or place too many hopes in the future, and supposedly unhealthy to dwell too much on the past . . .

But sometimes a little 'unhealthy' indulgence can be healing and revitalizing. Surely there is real joy in recalling times of happiness

I FEEL
LIKE
ENOCH
WHO
WALKED
WITH
GOD

The only sounds...
whispering wind,
murmur of sea...
a skylark

and bringing to mind people who have enriched our lives. It is one of the positive aspects of old age, that each of us possesses a storehouse of memories which can be delightful to draw on in the quiet hours. We may feel much sympathy for the old shepherd praying:

> Heavenly Master, I wud like to wake to they same green places
> Where I be know'd for breakin' dogs and follerin' sheep.
> And if I may not walk in th'old ways and look on th'old faces
> I wud sooner sleep.

CHARLOTTE MEW

Wine

Wine gives life if drunk in moderation.
What is life worth without wine?
It was created to make people happy.
(Ecclesiasticus 31.27)

Wine in a glass looks inviting, tastes good. It may lift my spirits, give me a headache, or make me ill. Is it wise to drink wine, or any alcohol?

It is interesting that some Christians look on the drinking of alcohol as a sin. John Wesley saw the effects of drink on the struggling poor and condemned it.

Yet we know that, as in the quotation above from Ecclesiasticus, the Old Testament gives wine a very positive press. In Psalm 104.14–15 we read:

> He causeth the grass to grow for the cattle, and herb for the service of man: that he may bring forth food out of the earth; and wine that maketh glad the heart of man, and oil to make his face to shine, and bread which strengtheneth man's heart.

Jesus himself not only drank wine but encouraged others to do so. At the wedding in Cana, he changed water into exceptionally high quality wine for the enjoyment of his friends: to make it a good party. And the night before he died, after he had given the cup to his friends, Jesus made his promise; 'From now on, I tell you, I shall never again drink wine until the day I drink the new wine with you in the kingdom of my Father.'

So there is to be wine-drinking in the Kingdom of Heaven.

Lord, help us not to be too puritannical in our attitude
towards alcohol,
but to feel free to enjoy a glass of wine in conviviality.
Help us also to be aware of the danger of drink
and sensitive to the frailty of those who become
addicted to alcohol.

Wood

Touch
wood

I look at the beautiful grain in the wood of the coffee-table my friend George Ineson made. I wonder about the tree it came from. It was an elm tree. At the time the table was carved, elm trees were dying all over England, and it seemed appropriate to ask George to create something lasting from this wood.

But there are things in my house made from trees that could be living still had they not been cut down to make stuff that nobody needs. There are cardboard containers for toothpaste, and a pile of 'junk mail', consisting mostly of leaflets which try to persuade me to spend money on yet more rubbish.

Most people know about the rain forests, and the terrible damage that is being done not only locally in the faraway places where the trees are being cut down, but ultimately to the whole planet. We may feel that any attempts that we may personally make, for example to put pressure on manufacturers to use less packaging or to learn about the comparative benefits of recycling waste, is merely a drop in the ocean—or a leaf in the rain forest—and therefore not worth the effort, or sometimes the extra cost involved.

But the fight to conserve the rain forests—the fight against the multinational companies and those who in greed exploit our natural resources—needs the united support of all those who care about the future of our world. We can educate ourselves to know what measures we *can* take in our own lives, to redress the balance.

Lord God, you made the universe
And saw that it was good.
You saw the brilliance of the stars,
The beauty of the flowers,

The far depths of the oceans,
The drama of the mountains,
The glory of the great, life-giving forests,
The wonderful variety of animals and birds,
The intelligence and potential of humankind,
You saw all this and saw that it was good.

But later you saw evil,
For man and woman
Misused their intelligence,
Misused their power.
They cut down the great trees
And robbed the forests of their glory,
Setting in motion
Famine, misery, and death.

> Lord, forgive us.
> Let us seize the chance,
> before it is too late,
> through the power of your Holy Spirit,
> to renew the face of the earth.

Wrapping Paper

Wrapping paper,
decorative or sturdy.
It's what's inside
that counts.

Now when I see a piece of wrapping paper, my thoughts turn at once to Ravensbruck. Like Auschwitz and Dachau, Ravensbruck is one of those places imprinted on the memory because of the horrors perpetrated there.

During the Second World War, in the concentration camp at Ravensbruck the most heinous crimes imaginable were committed by human beings against their brothers and sisters. Ninety-two thousand women and children died there. But it was also there that a piece of wrapping paper was found which bears testimony to the greatness of the human spirit. On it was written:

> O Lord,
> remember not only the men and women of goodwill,
> but also those of ill will.
> But do not only remember the suffering they have
> inflicted on us,
> remember the fruits we bore thanks to this suffering,
> our comradeship, our loyalty, our humility,
> the courage, the generosity,
> the greatness of heart which has grown out of all this.
> And when they come to judgement
> let all the fruits we have borne
> be their forgiveness. AMEN AMEN AMEN.

Such magnanimity is awe-inspiring. Those of us who lead quite ordinary, comfortable lives often find it difficult to forgive small hurts and unkindnesses. Sometimes it seems too much to expect those whose lives have been shattered—like the mothers of young children who have been raped or murdered—to offer forgiveness.

> Lord,
> I thank you for your words of forgiveness on the cross,
> for those who were torturing you.
> I thank you for those whose courage and greatness of heart
> inspire us.
> Let us be merciful,
> not only to those who offend us,
> but also to those who find forgiveness so difficult.

Child

As for you, little child,
you shall be called a
Prophet of God the Most High.
(Luke 1.76)

I don't suppose anyone will ever call little Jacob a prophet, but in a sense that is what he was. This morning I received a letter from his parents:

> We are sorry to say that on Friday 25th June at six o'clock in the morning, Jacob died peacefully at home. He set us a wonderful example of how to live and die and we feel much blessed.

Jacob died at the age of six after battling with leukaemia for years. He was a prophet because somehow, in his young life, he was able to interpret the will, the word, the love of God. Because of the way he was, and because of their own strong faith, his parents can be accepting and positive, although there is no doubt that their grief is very real.

How can it be that a little boy, not outstanding in any other way, should become such a blessing? My guess is that Jacob was not a child set apart, specially blessed by God from the beginning, but that he was born to parents of deep faith and commitment and he lived, much as Jesus must have done, in a family where each member has grown strong in reciprocal love.

One day, Isaiah's vision will be realized:

> The wolf lives with the lamb,
> the panther lies down with the kid,
> calf and lion cub feed together
> with a little boy to lead them.
> (Isaiah 11.6)

Then God's kingdom will have come and let us pray that all of us, like Jacob's family, will live together in mutual love.

Lord, I pray for all who mourn;
May they be comforted.
May they come to rejoice in the lives of those they have lost.
I thank you for Jacob.

Fledgling

The bird has
flown the nest.

I saw the fledgling from my window. It made a shaky start. I held my breath, afraid that it would fall. Then it steadied and with a swift, sure movement, soared upwards over the rooftops and was gone.

I wondered about the mother bird. Was she still sitting calm and unruffled upon the nest? I thought of my own children and I remembered the words of Kahlil Gibran:

Your children are not your children.
They are the sons and daughters of Life's longing for itself.
They came through you but not from you
And though they are with you they do not belong to you.

. . .

You are the bows from which your children as
living arrows are sent forth.

But it is not only our children that we need to let go. We lie awake at night, tossing and turning with worry over things beyond our control. We strive our utmost to find ways of solving problems, especially for those we love and want to help. We find it so hard to stand back, to let go and hand over not only our own lives, but the lives of our loved ones, in trust to God. It is difficult to let go, but worth it, because once we have let God take over we are free to walk serenely in his ways.

In Peter's first letter, he writes: 'Bow down, then, before the power of God now . . . unload all your worries on to him, since he is looking after you.' (1 Peter 5.6)

And the writer of Psalm 62 exhorts us to put our trust in God:

In God is my safety and glory,
the rock of my strength.
Take refuge in God, all you people.
Trust him at all times.
Pour out your hearts before him
for God is our refuge.

(Psalm 62.8)

Dear Lord, I pour out my heart before you,
I hand over all my anxieties,
my hopes and my life
into your care.

YOU
ARE
THE
BOW
from which your children as living arrows are
sent forth . . . Let your bending in the Archer's
hand be for gladness; for even as He loves the
arrow that flies, so He loves also the bow
that is stable. KAHLIL GIBRAN

Shoes

How beautiful are
thy feet with shoes,
O prince's daughter!
(Song of Solomon 7.1 AV)

'How beautiful these shoes are!' I think, when I try on a pair of new ones in the shop. I look down on the neat pair: shining, perfectly shaped, without a flaw. Then I glance sideways at the pair I have taken off, my old shoes. I wonder for a moment how I could have borne to be seen alive in them. They are badly scuffed, down at heel, misshapen.

But then I look again and see them in another light, with something like affection. They look as they do because they are worn to the shape of my feet. They are old and tired because I have tramped so many miles in them, on walks that have led me into all sorts of encounters and experiences.

Suddenly my shoes remind me of myself: not beautiful, not perfect, but rather battered and worn by life, and I begin to think of myself, too, with some affection.

The two great commandments of Jesus, to love God and love our neighbour as ourselves, are a tremendous challenge and they go on challenging us day after day. It is impossible to love God as he deserves to be loved; it is extremely difficult to love some of our neighbours. And what about the sting in the tail: *as yourself*? For some of us that is even harder.

To love myself: it goes against the grain, the grain of my formation as a Christian, it goes against all I have been taught about humility and self-denial and putting myself last.

Yet since God loves us so much, since we are made in his image and likeness, it follows that we are lovable. It is true that we are sinners, that we are weak, that we keep making the same mistakes over and over again, but it is also true that we are worthy of love.

And not only are we worthy of love, we need to take this truth on board and act on it if we sincerely want to serve God. I *have* to love myself, at least to some degree, if I am to succeed in loving my neighbour.

So I look at myself as I looked at my old shoes and see my limitations. I accept that I will never be perfect, that for all my striving I will continue to sin, to fail, to be weak. But that is me. There is no one else with my fingerprints, there is nobody quite like me. And for all my shabbiness, feebleness and imperfections, I thank God for the miracle that is me.

Some people find it difficult if not impossible to accept that they are lovable, to feel happy about themselves. Gerard Manley Hopkins wrote:

> My own heart let me have pity on; let
> Me live to my sad self hereafter kind.

Lord, you know the difficulty we have in loving ourselves.
Give us a deeper trust in you,
who made us,
who loves us unconditionally,
just as we are.
And so let us come to see ourselves as you see us:
lovable, loved, and capable of loving.

Rain

Rain, rain,
go away.
Come again
another day.

I do not like the rain. I do not like the leaden skies, the lack of light, the lack of colour. I hate carrying an umbrella, for fear I will put it down and lose it, or poke someone in the eye with one of the spokes. Because it is raining, the Test Match has been delayed, Wimbledon has been postponed, the summer fête is a wash-out and I am soaked to the skin.

Then I think of the children in the desert, the children who are near-skeletons, except for their swollen bellies. Their beautiful dark eyes are listless now. Too weak to stand or walk, they sit on the sand in long rows, completely silent. They are looking at the sky, because if the rain comes, they will be saved. They are longing for the rain.

Lord, send them rain.

In desert lands, rain brings life. So in the writings of the prophet Isaiah we read:

> Let the desert and the dry lands be glad,
> let the wasteland rejoice and bloom;
> like the asphodel, let it burst into flower,
> let it rejoice and sing for joy.
>
> . . .
>
> Then the eyes of the blind will be opened,
> the ears of the deaf unsealed,
> then the lame will leap like a deer
> and the tongue of the dumb sing for joy;
> for water will gush in the desert
> and streams in the wastelands.
>
> (Isaiah 35.1–2, 5–6)

Lord, send us rain.

LET THE DESERT AND
THE DRY LANDS BE
GLAD · LET THE WASTE
LAND REJOICE AND
BLOOM · LIKE THE ASP-
HODEL LET IT BURST
INTO FLOWER · LET IT
REJOICE AND SING FOR
JOY · THEN THE EYES OF
THE BLIND WILL BE
OPENED AND THE EARS
OF THE DEAF UNSEALED ·

THE LAME
WILL LEAP LIKE
THE DEER

THEN THE LAME WILL
LEAP LIKE THE DEER
AND THE TONGUE OF
THE DUMB SING FOR
JOY · FOR WATER WILL
GUSH IN THE DESERT

Table

The centre of the home
where everyone gathers
to share food and conversation,
to be family and welcome friends.

How blessed are all who fear Yahweh,
who walk in his ways!

. . .

Your wife is a fruitful vine
in the inner places of your house,
your children round your table
like shoots of an olive tree.
(Psalm 128.1, 3)

Life in our society has changed radically over the past two generations, for good as well as ill. One of the less happy changes is the disintegration of the family, and a symbol and symptom of this, in many cases, is the end of eating together round a table.

Nowadays individual members of a family often come in from school or work at different times, grab some food from the fridge, heat it up in a microwave oven and eat it on their laps in front of television. There is nothing wrong with refrigerators and microwaves, marvellous inventions both, and watching television *can* be beneficial. But people who have to live in this way, because of the pressures of life or simply because they have not experienced any other way, are missing something which is not just a sentimental tradition but a vital element in the upbuilding of family life.

The table was, and in some families still is, the focus

of living together. It is the place where food is shared and people relate to one another, the place for celebration. In church, the table of the Lord is the focus of worshipping together, the place where food is shared among the family gathered there, the place for celebration.

The ordinary table, in the kitchen or the living room, is not consecrated to God like the altar in church, but if it is the place where people meet together in love, then it is blessed by their presence and becomes holy.

Grace before Supper

O Lord Jesu Christ
without whom nothing is sweet nor savoury,
we beseech thee to bless us and our supper,
and with thy blessed presence to cheer our hearts,
that in all our meats and drinks,
we may savour and taste of thee,
to thy honour and glory.

Take away all coldness, all wanderings of thoughts and fix our souls upon thee

Chair

Everyone under his vine
and his fig tree.
(1 Kings 4.25)

Here is a picture of peace and simple contentment: the peasant sitting in the shade of his fruitful trees at the end of the day.

I have neither vine nor fig tree, but I do have a chair where I sit contentedly. When I want to pray I sit on this chair. It is an old red chair, once handsome, now shabby and still exceptionally comfortable. I can relax in my chair.

I think I pray most effectively when I am sitting. Painful knees and an aching back are distractions. But my chair is facing the window and unless I close my eyes I can see the flowers in the garden and the houses opposite. Perhaps they are distractions too, but I tend to see them as part of my prayer, because beauty never fails to lift my mind to God in praise, and the houses are the homes of my neighbours for whom I like to pray.

Sometimes, when I am praying in my chair, I also

listen to music. It soothes me or raises my spirits, but does not distract me from thoughts of God.

This is my way of praying, but I realize that for some people it would not be the 'right' way. They would feel it necessary to kneel in silence, in church perhaps, or in the most austere surroundings.

There is no absolute rule about where or how to pray. Each woman or man who longs to know God, to come closer to him and grow more like him, is free to find the way of praying that suits them best.

For me it is sitting in the red chair, looking out of the window, listening to inspiring music, and to God.

> O Lord, take away all coldness,
> all wanderings of the thoughts,
> and fix our souls upon thee and thy love,
> O merciful Lord and Saviour,
> in this our hour of prayer.
>
> EDWARD BENSON

Hoe

The cure for this ill is not to sit still,
Or frowst with a book by the fire;
But to take a large hoe and a shovel also
And dig till you gently perspire.

RUDYARD KIPLING

How strong are you? How healthy? Can you use a hoe or a spade? Are you capable of hard work?

There are some people who are wonderful. They keep going at work, even tough physical work, well into their seventies or even older. I knew a gardener, Mr Abel, who was still working full-time at eighty-five. Early retirement was not for the likes of him.

When we think of our grandmothers or great-grandmothers and the lives they led, we sometimes feel effete and inadequate. It was 'all in the day's work' for a mother of six children to walk a mile or so to a well for water twice a day, to wash all clothing and bedding by hand, to cook without benefit of

electricity or gas, to dig the garden . . . And nowadays almost all housework is done at the press of a button.

So why are we so feeble? Or is it feebleness?

In the past two generations, our lifestyle has changed dramatically. Nowadays most of us work much shorter hours and machinery has taken the place of hard manual labour. But life is no easier: mental and emotional strain take their toll on our bodies too. The pace of life is getting faster; relationships are complex and less stable.

Of course there has always been stress. The cavemen must have suffered from it, but not to the degree that we do today. So we are not feeble. Life is just as hard for us as it was for our forebears. Perhaps they went to bed with aching limbs; now we lie awake worrying.

Then, as now, 'all work and no play' made Jack a dull boy. Not only does it make us dull but weary too. All of us need space and rest: time to rest from digging and simply smell the roses, space to be happy 'frowsting' with a book by the fire.

Drop thy still dews of quietness,
Till all our strivings cease;
Take from our souls the strain and stress,
And let our ordered lives confess
The beauty of thy peace.

J.G. WHITTIER

Kiss

I was surprised when she kissed me, embarrassed too,
but then I realized that in that instant, acquaintance
had blossomed into friendship.

Many of us are shy about touching one another. We explain this as consistent with dignity and decent reserve.

But Jesus was highly sensitive to touch, and often touched people himself. Most moving is the account of his touching the leper, the outcast abhorred by everyone, and shunned as sometimes in our own day people with Aids are shunned.

In his second letter to the Corinthians, Paul wrote: 'Greet one another with the holy kiss' (2 Corinthians 13.12) and it is in response to this that nowadays in some of our Christian traditions people exchange the sign of peace in church. This is meant to show that we are brothers and sisters, belonging to a real community, loving one another.

But some people will go to extreme lengths to avoid physical contact with others. There is the story of the English lady who went to church in Ireland when the sign of peace was first introduced. Stiff as a ramrod, she looked down her nose at the unsuspecting man proffering his hand and said 'I'm British!'

We may laugh at such an attitude, or we may identify with this woman. From whatever cause, some of us have a deep-rooted fear of physical intimacy with those who are not close to us. It is only when we become convinced of the power of touch to bring trust and healing that we can find the courage to overcome this.

Many of us may be like 'old Mr Frost' in the following lines:

At the sign of peace
Old Mr Frost kept his hands stiff at his sides.
He averted his eyes from eager, well-meaning Judy
And flinched from the sticky fingers of little Wayne.

But when he felt the cool firm touch
Of Miss Paley's outstretched hand,
And saw her austere, plain face
Transformed by a smile,
He gave in.
He managed to take her hand,
He brought himself to answer her smile
And said, meaning it,
'Peace be with you.'

Lord, help us to respect the sensitivities of one another.
Help us to sense when the touch of a hand or a kiss or a hug would be acceptable,
and let us not be afraid to show spontaneity and affection.

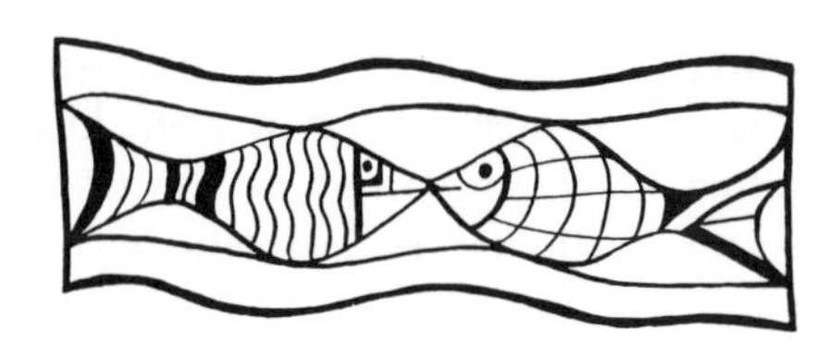

Cloth

A ragged piece of cloth, used for cleaning.
Holding it, I think of Veronica
who wiped blood, sweat and tears
from the face of Jesus.

Veronica is not to be found in Scripture. She is a legendary figure, but she stands for all the women who show tenderness to the suffering. She stands too for all those who dare to act alone, courageously.

At the end of the Second World War, word went through a Russian city that a column of German prisoners of war would be marching through the streets. Many women came to see. They lined the streets, waiting for the enemy to pass by. Their hearts were full of loathing and anger, because they were the mothers, wives, and sweethearts of men who had been killed by the Germans. They watched in silent hatred as the first group of men marched past, the officers in smart uniforms with proud arrogant faces.

But then, all at once, the whole atmosphere changed as the long line of ordinary soldiers straggled behind, some wounded, all thin and shabby, all wretched and hopeless, all hungry-looking.

Suddenly one woman stepped from the line of onlookers, walked up to a German soldier and offered him a crust of bread. Within moments every woman who had anything to give was giving it. The German soldiers were no longer the enemy.

When Jesus was in Bethany, eating a meal with his friends, a woman came with an alabaster jar of very costly ointment and poured it over his head. She was risking embarrassment and the censure of others, but Jesus praised her and said, 'In truth I tell you, wherever in all the world this gospel is proclaimed, what she has done will be told as well, in remembrance of her' (Matthew 26.13).

It may be interesting to ponder on the prayer of Margaret

Godolphin, and adapt it to our circumstances. Margaret was an unmarried girl of sixteen, maid of honour to Queen Catherine, wife of Charles the Second, when she wrote this. Evidently in her own narrow world she was a woman of great courage, not afraid to be different:

When I go into the withdrawing room,
let me consider what my calling is:
let me consider, if a Traitor be hateful,
she that betrays the soul of one is much worse,
the danger, the sin of it.
Then, without pretending to wit,
how quiet and pleasant a thing it is
to be silent, or if I do not speak,
that it be to the Glory of God. Lord, assist me.
If they speak of anybody I can't commend,
hold my peace what jest soever they make;

. . .

when they speak filthily,
tho' I be laughed at, look grave.
Never meddle with others' business,
nor hardly ask a question;
talk not slightly of religion.
If you speak anything they like,
say 'tis borrowed, and be humble when commended.
Before I speak, Lord, assist me;
when I pray, Lord, hear me;
when I am praised, God, humble me;
may the clock, the candle,
everything I see, instruct me;
Lord, cleanse my hands,
let my feet tread thy paths.

Song

This morning
there is a song in my heart.

There are some days when, whether we are tone deaf or not, we feel like singing: the sun is shining and we have good news. It is the sort of feeling we catch from Browning when he writes:

God's in his heaven—
All's right with the world!

The trouble is, all is definitely not right with the world, far from it. Nearly everything seems *wrong* with our world: famine, war, greed, torture, the lust for power, the wanton destruction of creation. Should we not therefore be crying rather than singing?

It is a paradox that the true Christian, who is compassionate, 'feeling with' all who suffer, is also unfailingly joyful. Deep within us, the Holy Spirit is a well-spring of joy.

George Fox, founder of the Society of Friends, understood this. He wrote: 'Walk cheerfully over the world, answering that of God in everyone.'

Jesus wanted us to share fully in his joy (John 17.13), and Paul wrote to the Philippians saying,

> I want you to be happy, always happy in the Lord; I repeat, what I want is your happiness. Let your tolerance be evident to everyone: the Lord is very near. There is no need to worry; but if there is anything you need, pray for it, asking God for it with prayer and thanksgiving, and that peace of God, which is so much greater than we can understand, will guard your hearts and your thoughts, in Christ Jesus.
>
> (Philippians 4.4–8)

That seems like a wonderful prescription for happiness, and perhaps in response to it we should sing not only in the sunshine but in the rain. Naturally, and importantly, we grieve in our sadness, for the personal tragedies of those we know and for the sufferings of victims the world over. Sometimes it seems as though we are weighed down by cares and sorrows. But for those who believe in the love of God, the resurrection of Jesus and the kingdom that is to come, the song within us can never be completely silenced.

O sing a new song to the Lord,
sing to the Lord all the earth.
O sing to the Lord, bless his name.
(Psalm 96.1)

Neighbour

There goes my neighbour. I used to dislike her,
but since I tried to love her I have begun to like her.

Who is my neighbour? My neighbour is the one Jesus asks me to love. He may be the man next door, she may be someone I have never seen, who lives on the other side of the world and needs my prayers. He may be a dear friend, or someone I bump into in the street or the supermarket, meet on a train. She may be someone I see in a refugee camp on television. My neighbour is someone whose life touches mine.

Jesus said, 'I tell you solemnly, in so far as you did this to one of the least of these brothers of mine, you did it to me' (Matthew

25.40). The implication for those who try to follow him is that we should treat everyone we meet as we would Jesus and try to see him in our neighbour.

Some people are easy to like and love but often it is a struggle for all of us to respect and reverence certain people who cross our path.

Donald Nicholl tells of his experience in an American jail. He had become a prison visitor, and after one or two visits had begun to feel affection for the particular inmate allotted to him. Then he made the mistake of asking 'What are you in for?'

Donald was prepared to hear that it was for robbery, or violence, or even murder, but when the prisoner, Mike, told him it was for peddling drugs, he confesses he was shocked because he had always felt that he could cheerfully strangle anyone who peddled drugs. He heard himself saying to himself 'I didn't sign up for this!'

Then he looked up and saw Christ gazing at him over Mike's shoulder. Christ said, 'And who are you to decide who is to be saved or not?'

As followers of Christ in our crowded, secular, sophisticated world, we wrestle with the problems of relating to others. It is refreshing to reflect on the words of an Irish farmer who lived centuries ago in a quite different world:

> I saw a stranger yestreen.
> I put food in the eating place,
> Drink in the drinking place,
> Music in the listening place.
> And in the sacred name of the Triune
> He blessed me and my house,
> My cattle and my dear ones.
> And the lark said in her song:
> 'Often, often, often,
> Goes the Christ in the stranger's guise.'

We may smile at the priority given to the cows, but at the same time long to emulate the wisdom and simplicity of one who with such clear eyes sees the Lord Jesus in the stranger, his neighbour.

Lord, teach me to find you in everyone who crosses my path.

Silence

Silence enfolds me
like some benign presence,
like God himself.

Elected Silence, sing to me
And beat upon my whorlèd ear,
Pipe me to pastures still and be
The music that I came to hear.
GERARD MANLEY HOPKINS

Silence singing? As so often in his poetry Hopkins surprises us. But these lines have the ring of truth and of experience. In the deepest silence, there is a kind of music. I have heard it when walking alone in the Cheviot hills, in moments when no sheep were bleating, no skylarks trilling, no jets zooming overhead. And I have heard it when I have been part of a small group of women, together in silent, concentrated prayer.

For me, it is worth the struggle of getting up early in the morning before the bustle of the day begins, to sit in complete silence alone, waiting on God.

In silence there is a sense of expectancy. Passive, receptive, we wait for a word, a thought, a revelation, and if none of these comes to us we stay tranquil, resting with God, enjoying his presence.

In silence there is healing. One by one we let go of the peripheral concerns of our life, and petty distractions and anxieties, and allow God to take over and hold us so that for a while our pain is numbed.

It is said of the mother of Jesus, that amidst all the activity surrounding his birth, 'Mary kept all these things, and pondered them in her heart' (Luke 2.19 AV).

She knew the value of silence, as do the Society of Friends, the

Quakers, whose founder, George Fox, wrote: 'Be still and cool in thy own mind and spirit from thy own thoughts, and then thou wilt feel the principle of God to turn thy mind to the Lord God.'

> Lord, you have said,
> 'Be still and know that I am God.'
> Help us to find you in the stillness of our bodies
> and the silence of our hearts.

Purify me with hyssop till
I am clean, wash me till I am
whiter than snow

PSALM 51

Soap

Cleanliness is, indeed,
next to godliness.
JOHN WESLEY

The soap in my bathroom is green to match the décor and it smells of flowers. But I look at the row of bottles and jars on the bathroom shelf: at the moisturizer, the deodorant, the talcum powder, the bathfoam, all prettily packaged and smelling nice, and I begin to wonder, have we gone a bit too far? Has cleanliness overtaken godliness in our present-day western culture? Do I really need all this stuff?

I wonder what Jesus would make of it all. He certainly didn't use conditioner in his hair. Did Mary Magdalene use a skin freshener? Of course it is not a fair comparison, because we have certainly moved on in technical advances and sophistication over the past two thousand years, and our culture is entirely different from that of first-century Palestine. But even so, isn't it possible that we spend too much time and money and thought on how we look and how we smell?

We could choose a different priority. We could echo the heartfelt cry of the writer of Psalm 51:

> Purify me with hyssop till I am clean,
> wash me till I am whiter than snow.
> (Psalm 51.7)

He was not thinking of the cleansing of his body. His anxiety was for the purity of his soul. And we, instead of worrying about acne, or dandruff, or broken nails, could be concerned with our dishonesty, and pettiness, and unkindness. An obsession with sin and guilt is unhealthy and counter-productive, but a clear honest look at ourselves and a longing for purity of heart will bring us closer to God.

Later in the same psalm we read, 'O God, create in me a clean heart.'

Let us forget the enriching, revitalizing night cream and make this our prayer instead.

Toothache

There was never yet philosopher
That could endure the toothache patiently.
SHAKESPEARE

How can it be that it always seems to be Friday night when I get a raging toothache? I will have to live through the agony till Monday morning, and nothing seems to help, not painkillers, or cottonwool soaked in whisky, and certainly not a pious friend who advises me to 'offer it up'. I don't want to offer it up; I want it to go away. Another good Christian suggests that I think about the sufferings of Jesus on the cross, but somehow even that does nothing for the pain in my tooth. I pray to God to take the pain away, but he does nothing.

In the scale of suffering, compared to starvation, torture, the death of a child, or a broken relationship, toothache counts as nothing. That God does not interfere to end our grief and pain, is for some the most incomprehensible thing of all and the greatest stumbling-block to faith. If he is a loving God, then why, oh why does he fail to rescue us in our distress and feed us in time of famine?

We have to face the truth that it is a rarity for God to deliver us from suffering. But how can a compassionate God stand by and do nothing while his creatures writhe in physical, mental, emotional, or spiritual agony; when people, good people who love him, cry out to him for pity?

Some people have tried to explain God's apparent deafness by saying that it is all our own fault, that most of the suffering is caused, directly or indirectly, by us human beings. Since he has given us free will, they argue, God cannot interfere when we choose to maim or kill or starve our fellow creatures.

But this is no real answer to the problem. Human beings do not cause earthquakes. They are not to blame when a child is born deformed or a loved one dies of cancer.

I believe that creation is flawed. God's kingdom has not yet come, the wolf does not yet lie down with the lamb, the calf and the lion cub do not feed together. They hurt and destroy on the holy mountain of the Lord.

And our God is all-loving but he is not all-powerful, not in the sense that he can stop the world and put an end to suffering. He is himself the one who suffers most.

I also believe that God is with us in every situation, sharing our pain (even our toothache!) because he is love itself. He is not deaf to our cries; he hears, he listens, he is there, holding us fast.

He is like the mother who silently feels the pain of her child. He will never forsake us. Jesus has promised:

> Know that I am with you always;
> yes, to the end of time.
> (Matthew 28.20)

May Jesus Christ, the King of Glory,
help us to make the right use
of all the suffering that comes to us,
and offer to him the incense
of a patient and trustful heart;
for his Name's sake. Amen.

JOHANN TAULER

Nail

> *Unless I see the holes that the nails made in his hands . . .*
> *I refuse to believe.*
>
> (John 20.25)

The nail is rusty, but still sharp. Looking at it, I think of Jesus, nailed so cruelly, through his hands and his feet, to the cross. Then I think of all those through history and in our own day who suffer torture.

For most of us, happily, torture is something never likely to happen to us and beyond our imagining. What was it like to be hanged, drawn and quartered? What is it like to live for months in solitary confinement? Listening to the experience of hostages like Brian Keenan and Terry Waite is not the same as living through it ourselves. And what of all those, so many of them nameless ones, who have to suffer torture today in places where human rights are denied?

It could be argued that this is something that we don't need to think about at all. Isn't it akin to watching horror films or enjoying scenes of violence on television? Can we not simply be thankful that it does not happen to us and shut it out of our minds?

Well, the problem is that the victims of torture—and the perpetrators— are our brothers and sisters. Like it or not, torture *is* our concern.

Prisoners of conscience the world over have testified to the support they have felt through the prayers of others— people they will never meet. There is power in prayer, and power, too, in the work of Amnesty International. Though not a Christian organization, Amnesty fulfils the commands of Christ to love and serve one another, by identifying the abuse of human rights and using every possible means to end it.

Lord, enliven our imaginations
and sharpen our sensibilities
so that we may grasp the reality of what is happening
to innocent victims in different countries in our world.
Through the power of your Holy Spirit,
let our response be a willingness
to become involved with those who suffer in this way,
by prayer and action.

Lord
enliven our
imagination
and sharpen
our sensibilities
so that we may
grasp the real-
ity of what is
happening to
innocent people
in other parts
of the world.

Recipe

> *By carefully reading the Recipes there should not be the slightest difficulty in arranging a repast for any number of persons.*
>
> ISABELLA BEETON

I lost the recipe for my Christmas cake. That may not seem like a major tragedy, but I was distraught. It was a very special recipe, handed down to me from my great-great-grandmother, and I had been making that cake every year for as long as I could remember.

It was always a success: it looked wonderful, smelt wonderful and tasted even better. But although I turned the house upside-down, I could not find my recipe.

At first I was in despair. I considered having no cake, or, perhaps worse, a bought one. But then I pulled myself together. I realized that there are a lot of good recipes for Christmas cakes, and that even if I couldn't remember the fine nuances of that particular one, I could surely make a decent Christmas cake for my family. And so I did. Someone even pronounced it 'the best ever'!

Even so, I couldn't help feeling sad that a little piece of family tradition was lost. The idea of holding on to the past appeals to me, and this doesn't only apply to recipes and photographs and letters and the like; it applies to my faith too.

I find it hard that we so seldom hear the beautiful language of the Authorized Version any more. I find it hard to join enthusiastically in choruses which seem to me banal both in word and music. There have been times when change has seemed like the beginning of the end, as though the whole fabric of the Church would crumble because a well-loved prayer is no longer included in the liturgy.

It took me a while to realize that without change we can neither live nor grow. Our conception of the Church and of faith itself has to change in order to meet the needs of the people of God. I must have not only an open mind but a sense of proportion, so that I can see that the baby is quite safe while the bath water runs down the plughole.

We can celebrate a happy Christmas without the cake made from my treasured recipe, and God's Church will survive all the adaptations and changes we make. Without losing our respect for those who have gone before us, keeping the faith alive and alight, we can cheerfully embrace the new ideas and new attitudes that come from those who today hold God central in their lives.

Lord, let us not cling to those things which have outlived
their value.
Help us to walk in newness of life,
welcoming every change
which hastens the coming of your kingdom.

Clothes

The apparel oft
proclaims the man.
SHAKESPEARE

To look at a line of washing tossing on a sunny day is highly satisfactory for the one who did the washing, and no small pleasure for me, just looking. Seeing the line of assorted garments my mind jumps to think of the younger generation. Why? Because their clothes are so much prettier than ours used to be: the fabrics lighter, the colours brighter. I see the tiny flower-sprigged briefs—how can anybody fit into them?—and remember that, when I was young in the 'good' old days, all of us girls wore navy blue knickers with elastic tightly gripping our thighs. The little boys' shirts and trousers dancing in the breeze have cheerful patterns in every colour of the rainbow and more. Little boys in my day wore grey, full stop.

All this reminds me that not everything has changed for the worse. I suppose the older generation has always deplored the tastes and habits of the younger. Probably Adam and Eve grumbled endlessly about Abel and Cain. But I would like to wave a flag for the young, for the generation born after mine into a troubled and violent world.

The young so often get a bad press: it is the so-called joyriders and muggers we see on television news. Yet when thousands of young people visited London for the Taizé meeting in the late eighties, and prayed and sang together for hours, there was scarcely a mention of the event in the media.

When we listen to young people we can learn from them. They may not have such nice manners as we did, but they are often more honest, more open, more courageous, and more compassionate. Instead of accepting without question the faith of their forebears, they make a genuine search for meaning in their lives and sometimes they find God.

So I look at the cheerful line of clothes on the washing line, and I look to the future in the hands of our young people, with a measure of confidence and hope.

At Pentecost, when the disciples were filled with the Holy Spirit, Peter spoke to the crowds with a message from God:

> I shall pour out my Spirit on all humanity.
> Your sons and daughters shall prophesy,
> your young people shall see visions,
> your old people dream dreams.
>
> (Acts 2.17)

Lord, I pray for the young people of our world today.
Give them a vision which is your vision
so that there may be peace and justice in our world.

Dance

On with the dance! Let joy be unconfined.
BYRON

Just occasionally, when no one is looking, I dance. It is rather like singing in the bath. It doesn't matter that we can't sing or dance well; we do it for the sheer joy of living.

Dance is a powerful language, sometimes expressing far more than words. We have only to think of ballet dancers, whose graceful movements are full of meaning.

Nearer home, watch people at a barn dance. The most unlikely people, old, fat, normally staid, leap around the floor, their faces flushed with delight, their inhibitions forgotten. In dance they are able to let go, to release their feelings, to become free. Not even alcohol has such power.

A considerable number of people object to dancing in church. They feel that the building is a solemn place where everything must be dignified, that God will somehow be offended if we don't behave with decorum. Perhaps they forget that David the king danced before the Lord with all his might (2 Samuel 6.14). It was his way of expressing all that he felt for God.

We have much to learn from our brothers and sisters in the Pentecostal and other 'new' churches, where joy in praising God is unconfined and dancing is its natural expression.

It may have been David the king who wrote Psalm 30, ending with a joyful prayer of praise:

> You have turned my mourning into dancing,
> you have stripped off my sackcloth and clothed me with joy.
> So my heart will sing to you unceasingly,
> Yahweh, my God, I shall praise you for ever.
> (Psalm 30.11–12)

YOU HAVE TURNED MY MOURNING INTO

Wage Packet

Wage packet on the table
Not redundant then?
Not yet.

What does it mean, to be out of work, unemployed?

For some it means disaster, because they are already in debt, because the benefits allowed them by the state may cover only their basic needs: no more holidays, no more presents, a continued struggle to make both ends meet.

For some it means shame and humiliation. The work ethic is so strong that to be without work feels like disgrace.

For some it means a loss of dignity and pride and responsibility and achievement. They are convinced that they are failures.

There are a few who are glad not to work. They prefer to be idle and depend on the state for their upkeep.

And there are others, still fewer, who can find peace when they are out of work, by living frugally, finding pleasure in the simplest things, discovering their own creativity, enjoying freedom and unaffected by the work ethic.

How would these different people react on reading Psalm 128?

> How blessed are all who fear Yahweh,
> who walk in his ways!
> Your own labours will yield you a living,
> happy and prosperous you will be.
> (Psalm 128.1–2)

Unemployment is a huge problem in our day. Being out of work affects people differently. Often, those who have applied in vain for hundreds of jobs sink into apathy or despair. For some, the loss of self-esteem is the hardest to bear, for others it is the effect on their families.

Those of us who are in secure work usually feel powerless to help. Where we see injustice, we may be willing to become politically involved. There are possibilities of work-sharing, where one person does only half their normal hours of work for half their normal pay, so that someone else can benefit, and some people may be willing to consider retiring early so that others may take their job.

Lord, keep us aware of your presence throughout the day.
Help us to be grateful when we are able to work,
and to give of our best in all we do.
Lord, be with us when we are out of work.
Give us a sense of our own worth,
and keep us from depression and despair.

Wind

Who walketh upon the wings of the wind.
(Psalm 104.3)

I like to feel the wind on my face, to see the trees tossing, hair blowing, waves leaping over the rocks at the seaside. I like to listen to the wind when I am safe in bed at night. And I like to let my imagination run free when I think of the wind.

The wind features dramatically in Scripture. In Psalm 104, which extols the glories of creation, we are told that God walks on the wings of the wind. At Pentecost, when the Spirit of God descended upon the disciples, the sign that heralded his coming was a mighty rushing wind. In fact, in Greek and Hebrew, the languages in which the Bible was written, the same word means both 'spirit' and 'wind'.

To Nicodemus, Jesus says,

> The wind blows wherever it pleases;
> you hear its sound,
> but you cannot tell where it comes from
> or where it is going.
> That is how it is with all who are born
> of the Spirit.
>
> (John 3.8)

It seems to me that this is one of the key passages of Scripture. No one can harness the wind, still less can anyone confine the Holy Spirit of God.

He—or she—is free. That is why love and honesty and courage sometimes flower in those who do not know God. That is why Christians cannot rightly claim that theirs is the only acceptable way to worship. That is why no religion can be the sole repository of truth.

Many of us who are Christians are guilty of some degree of

intolerance towards those of other traditions, indulging in inter-denominational squabbles instead of rejoicing in the richness of our diversity. And many of us who are Christians are also guilty of arrogance and ignorance in our attitude towards those of other faiths, questioning their validity instead of revering their sincerity and holiness.

> Breathe on me, Breath of God,
> Fill me with life anew.
>
> EDWIN HATCH

Picture

Every picture
tells a story.
ANON

There is a picture on my wall which seems to tell a story. It shows a pretty bird flying with a twig in its beak. But the bird is blue and yellow and orange, so it is not a dove; and the twig bears a round yellow fruit, so it is not an olive branch.

The picture seems to be something of an allegory. It challenges me to ask: how real is the peace that I feel?

Early in the morning I sit in my chair and pray. I listen to God and rest in his presence. I am at peace.

> Truly I have set my soul
> in silence and in peace.
> A weaned child on its mother's breast,
> even so is my soul.
>
> (Psalm 131.2)

This beautiful psalm is a sort of idyll. Sadly, the peace I feel in my heart and in my home can only be fleeting. How can this be, for we are quiet people who abhor violence and love one another? But we are not at peace, because our world is ravaged by violence and war. When one part of the body is hurt, the rest is affected. As long as there are perpetrators of violence in any country, as long as nation is warring against nation, there can be no peace anywhere.

But paradoxically, we have to fight for peace, we have to be concerned for the victims of war, involved with those who work for justice. Peace may have to begin with me, but it will not come to me until the kingdom of peace has come into the world, and Isaiah's prophecy is fulfilled:

> They shall beat their swords into plowshares,
> and their spears into pruninghooks:
> nation shall not lift up sword against nation,
> neither shall they learn war any more.
> (Isaiah 2.4 AV)

O Lord, count us among the peacemakers.

Drainpipe

Make me a channel of your peace
attributed to
ST FRANCIS OF ASSISI

I am growing a rose up the drainpipe to disguise it a little, since it is not in itself a pretty object. Not pretty, but useful, until its channel gets blocked, that is.

I know that I could be a channel myself, a channel of God's love. But I, too, get blocked, mainly when I become absorbed in my own narrow concerns. Eric Hague tells the story of Bamboo. We hear how the Master of the Garden cut down this beautiful tree, Bamboo, stripped him of his leaves and branches and cut out his heart. He gently carried Bamboo to a spring of water in the middle of his fields and laid him down to make a channel so that the water from the spring could flow to irrigate the fields. Then rice was planted and grew vigorously until the day of the harvest came.

> In that day was Bamboo, once so glorious in stately beauty, yet more glorious in his brokenness and humility. For in his beauty was life abundant, but in his brokenness he became a channel of abundant life to his Master's world.
>
> ERIC HAGUE

The process of becoming open to the outpouring of God's love almost always involves first being in some way broken. This is because we have to change and be converted away from our consuming self-interest. Through fear, through habit, through the single-minded pursuit of success or power or money we can block the action of the Holy Spirit within us.

It is a strange paradox that God, whom we name the Almighty, needs us. If only we can empty ourselves of the obstacles which prevent us from working for him, we can become his instruments in this world, the channels through which his love and peace can flow to reach others.

As St Teresa said:

> Christ has no body now on earth but yours,
> no hands but yours,
> no feet but yours.
> Yours are the eyes through which must look out
> Christ's compassion on the world.
> Yours are the feet with which
> he is to go about doing good.
> Yours are the hands with which
> he is to bless people now.

Lord, help me.
Lord, use me.

Sir more than kisses letters mingle souls

Letter

Sir, more than kisses,
letters mingle souls.
JOHN DONNE

I saw it at once as it lay on the doormat among the junk mail and the bills. I recognized the handwriting on the fat white envelope—it was a letter from an old friend.

I picked it up and tore it open. Then, forgetting my breakfast, I sat down and read it. Sometimes I laughed out loud, sometimes tears sprang to my eyes. When I had finished the letter, I read it again more slowly.

It is a joy to receive letters from our good friends. Especially nowadays when people move around so much, it is a consolation to keep in touch by letter with those whose friendship we prize. The telephone, too, can be a lifeline for friendships, but it hardly 'mingles souls' in the way that letters sometimes can.

To have a good friend, someone with whom we can be ourselves and share our deepest concerns, is one of the greatest blessings in life. Distance and a long absence will not diminish a friendship like this, but a letter from such a friend always brings delight.

Some of the most powerful letters ever written came

from St Paul. We can imagine how eagerly the Romans, Corinthians, Ephesians, Galatians and the rest received and read them. Paul does a great deal of admonishing in his letters but he is also tender and affectionate towards his friends.

At the beginning of his letter to the Philippians he writes:

> I thank my God whenever I think of you; and every time I pray for all of you, I pray with joy . . . You have a permanent place in my heart, and God knows how much I miss you all.
>
> (Philippians 1.3, 7–8)

Lord, I thank you for my friends.
Help me to value them
and keep a permanent place for them in my heart.
I pray for all those who have no friends.

Clock

My clock is old
my clock is always slow
but the gentle rhythm of its tick
calms and soothes me.

Hurry, like noise, is the enemy of peace and holiness. Time should be savoured, used wisely, never wasted.

Early one morning, John, a friend of mine, came across an old man fishing in the River Esk. John, himself a fisherman, said, 'What a lovely way to waste time.'

But the old Yorkshireman answered gravely: 'Ah'm not wasting time. Ah'm fishing. There'll be plenty of time for wasting time when we're six feet under.'

As the wise fisherman knew, time is precious, and we do well to treasure every moment of our lives and put it to good use.

We may question *how* we spend our time. The Welsh poet W.H. Davies asks:

What is this life, if full of care
we have no time to stand and stare?

It is good to 'stand and stare' if we are engaged in fruitful meditation, and if we are simply enjoying a pause in our lives for quiet and rest or the contemplation of something beautiful. On the other hand there is a danger of *wasting* time if we spend it staring at those television programmes which are both worthless and boring, or listening to malicious gossip.

For the lonely and the bereaved, for those who care at home for long-term invalids, time moves all too slowly. The lives of others are so cluttered that the months seem to flash by and there is no time to take breath, to take stock of who they are and where they are going.

Lord, help me to appreciate your gift of time,
and to recognize its healing power.
Let me give my own time gladly
for your glory and the welfare of others.

Handbag

Not elegant,
but familiar
and above all,
capacious:
my handbag.

My handbag holds everything but the kitchen sink: well, not quite. And since I carry it everywhere with me, it feels almost like an old friend.

Inside it are 'essentials' and 'treasures'. The essentials are my glasses, purse, credit and donor cards, pen and notebook, comb, shopping list, paracetamols and diary. The treasures are photographs, letters, a marble a child once gave me, and a snippet of poetry or prayer that currently appeals to me. People sometimes ask: if your house was on fire and you could only save one thing, what would it be? I suppose in my case it would have to be my handbag.

That starts me wondering. Do I really need much more than the contents of my handbag? Over a lifetime I seem to have collected so many *things*: pictures, ornaments, and books. They give me pleasure and inspiration, but perhaps the time has come to stop and admit: enough is enough. I don't need any more possessions. I don't even want them any more.

I would like to live simply now, and to travel light—just me and my handbag. After all, Mother Teresa provides her sisters with just two saris and a bucket. And to his disciples, setting off for the first time as missionaries, Jesus said:

Provide yourselves with no gold or silver, not even with a few coppers for your purses, with no haversack for the journey or spare tunic or footwear or a staff, for the workman deserves his keep. (Matthew 10.9)

Perhaps I could even manage without my handbag?
NO!

Lord, teach me discernment.
Teach me to know myself.
Keep me open to the promptings of your Holy Spirit
so that my thinking and my actions
may be in tune with your will for me.

Night Sky

Twinkle, twinkle, little star
How I wonder what you are.

When I was a small child I used to sing this rhyme, but I never wondered *what* a star was, I only wondered at its beauty.

I have a clear memory of walking up the lane to my house one night with my mother and sister. I suppose I was about seven, and it was exciting to be out in the dark. The sky was alive with stars—hundreds, no, thousands of them—and I was astonished by their brilliance, awestruck.

When the first men landed on the moon I was quite grown-up. I was impressed like everyone else by the achievement, but part of me was saddened too. The moon had lost its mystery and magic.

For all this, nothing has been taken away from the loveliness of the moon: the great orange harvest moon hanging just above the horizon like a huge round lantern, the high silver moon seeming to scud along fast among the clouds, the still moon reflected in the calm water of a lake.

I have no wish to study astronomy. My star-gazing is a prayer of adoration to God who made the night sky. For me, and I think for all of us, it is vital to hold on to our sense of wonder, and not discard it with our belief in the man in the moon.

> Praised be thou, O Lord, for Sister Moon and
> the Stars, For that thou madest them clear, precious
> and lovely.
>
> Francis of Assisi

Blanket

In his love
he wraps and holds us.
He enfolds us for love
and he will never let us go
JULIAN OF NORWICH

A blanket is for wrapping us round, enfolding us. It is a homely symbol of the love of a mother for her child, and of God's love for us.

All of us—including the most sophisticated, the most successful, the most confident, and the most holy—need to know and to feel that we are loved. We need this, just as the homeless tramp needs warmth and comfort in the poem, 'The Embankment':

O God, make small
The old star-eaten blanket of the sky,
That I may fold it round me and in comfort lie.
T.E. HULME

It is tender love that we seek and need and long for when we cannot find it—the love of a father tucking up his small son at bedtime. And if we can only believe, such love is there for the asking, for each of us.

It is a sad truth that quite a number of people, even those who have been faithful, practising Christians all their lives, find it hard to accept that there can be such freely offered love. Sometimes it may be that they have never experienced true human love. Sometimes their image of God is that of a hard taskmaster, demanding perfection of them. And sometimes they simply cannot perceive of themselves as being worthy of love.

Yet Yahweh, our heavenly father, says to his people:

Does a woman forget her baby at the breast,
or fail to cherish the son of her womb?
Yet even if these forget,
I will never forget you.
See, I have branded you on the palms of my hands.
(Isaiah 49.15–16)

Abba, Father.
Help us to trust and to believe
in your everlasting, unconditional love
for each one of us.

SOURCES

All biblical references are from the Jerusalem Bible, unless otherwise indicated.

Preface
Aurora Leigh, VII: Elizabeth Barrett Browning, 1806–61.

Morning
The Christian Year 'Morning': John Keble, 1792–1866.
'God's Grandeur': Gerard Manley Hopkins, 1844–89.

Cup
Matthew 10.42 from The New Jerusalem Bible.
Alcuin, *c.* 735–804.

Sun
'I believe', lines written on a wall by a Jewish prisoner in Cologne.
'The True Son': Erasmus, 1466–1546.

Chain
'And can it be . . .?': Charles Wesley, 1707–88.

Garden
'God's Garden': Dorothy Gurney, 1858–1932.
'Thoughts in a Garden': Andrew Marvell, 1621–78.

Needle
Psalm 103.1–2 from the Grail Version.

Children
'Intimations of Immortality': William Wordsworth, 1770–1850.
John 1.47 from The New Jerusalem Bible.

Dead Bird
William Blake, 1757–1827.

Weed
Fortune of the Republic, Ralph Waldo Emerson, 1803–82.
1 Corinthians 13.6–7 from The New Jerusalem Bible.

Daisy
'Caribbean Woman Prayer': Grace Nichols, b. 1950: permission of Curtis Brown Ltd.
Luke 12.7 from the Authorized Version.

Dust
A prayer by John Donne, 1572–1637.

Crumb
'Jubilate Agno' Fragment B.1.154: Christopher Smart, 1722–71.
Isaiah 58.7–8 from The New Jerusalem Bible.

Cream
'King of Glory, King of Peace': George Herbert, 1593–1633.

Home
'The Maid of Milan': John Howard Payne, 1791–1852.
Psalm 84 from the Grail Version.

Flame
Quotation 'Come, thou Father': attributed to Archbishop Langton, 1150–1228.
Quotation 'Come Holy Ghost': attributed to Rabanus Maurus, 776–856.

Bible
The Ecclesiastical History of the English People, Bede, 673–735.
Psalm 143.8 from the Grail Version.

Walking-stick
'Old Shepherd's Prayer': Charlotte Mew, 1869–1928.

Wine
Ecclesiasticus 31.27 from The New Jerusalem Bible.
Psalm 104.14–15 from the Authorized Version.

Child
Luke 1.76 from the Grail Version.

Fledgling
The Prophet, Kahlil Gibran, 1883–1931.
Psalm 62.8 from the Grail Version.

Shoes
Gerard Manley Hopkins, 1844–89.

Rain
Isaiah 35.1–2, 5–6 from The New Jerusalem Bible.

Table
Psalm 128.1, 3 from The New Jerusalem Bible.
'Grace before Supper' from the *Primer of 1545*.

Chair
1 Kings 4.25 from The New Jerusalem Bible.
A prayer by Edward Benson, 1829–96.

Hoe
'How the Camel Got his Hump': *Just So Stories*, Rudyard Kipling, 1865–1936.
The second verse from the hymn 'Dear Lord and Father of mankind': by John Greenleaf Whittier, 1807–92.

Song
'Morning', *Pippa Passes*: Robert Browning, 1812–89.
Journal: George Fox, 1624–91.
Psalm 96.1 from the Grail version.

Silence
'The Habit of Perfection': Gerard Manley Hopkins, 1844–89.
Journal, George Fox, 1624–91.
'Be still and know that I am God': Psalm 46.9.

Soap
'On Dress', *Sermons*, xciii, John Wesley, 1703–91.

Toothache
Much Ado about Nothing, V, i, 35, William Shakespeare, 1564–1616.
A prayer, adapted, by Johann Tauler, *c.*1300–1361.

Recipe
Book of Household Management: Isabella Beeton, 1836–65.

Clothes
Hamlet, I, iii, 72, William Shakespeare, 1564–1616.

Dance
Childe Harold's Pilgrimage, I, iii, 24, George Gordon Byron, 1788–1824.
Psalm 30.11–12 from the Grail Version.

Wage Packet
Psalm 128.1–2 from The New Jerusalem Bible.

Wind
Psalm 104.3 from the Authorized Version.
Lines from the hymn 'Breathe on me, Breath of God': Edwin Hatch, 1835–89.

Picture
Psalm 131.2 from the Grail Version.

Drainpipe
Quotation 'Make me a channel': attributed to Francis of Assisi, 1181–1226.
In the Shadow of the Nine Dragons (CMS), Eric Hague.
Poem by Teresa of Avila, 1512–82.

Letter
'To Sir Henry Wotton': John Donne, 1572–1631.

Clock
'Leisure': W.H. Davies, 1871–1940.

Night Sky
'The Star', *Rhymes for the Nursery*, Jane Tylor, 1783–1824.
'Canticle of the Sun': Francis of Assisi, 1181–1226.

Blanket
Revelations of Divine Love: Julian of Norwich, *c.* 1342–1416.
'The Embankment': T.E. Hulme, 1883–1917.

Also published by

TRIANGLE

The PRAYING WITH series
A series of books making accessible the words of some of the great characters and traditions of faith for use by all Christians. There are 13 titles in the series, including:

PRAYING WITH SAINT AUGUSTINE
Introduction by Murray Watts

PRAYING WITH SAINT FRANCIS
Introduction by David Ford

PRAYING WITH HIGHLAND CHRISTIANS
Introduction by Sally Magnusson

PRAYING WITH THE NEW TESTAMENT
Introduction by Joyce Huggett

PRAYING WITH SAINT TERESA
Introduction by Elaine Storkey

PRAYING WITH THE JEWISH TRADITION
Introduction by Lionel Blue

PRAYING WITH THE OLD TESTAMENT
Introduction by Richard Holloway

PRAYING WITH THE ENGLISH HYMN WRITERS
Compiled and Introduced by Timothy Dudley-Smith

PRAYING WITH THE ENGLISH MYSTICS
Compiled and Introduced by Jenny Robertson

PRAYING WITH THE ENGLISH TRADITION
Compiled by Margaret Pawley
Preface by Robert Runcie

PRAYING WITH THE ENGLISH POETS
Compiled and Introduced by Ruth Etchells

PRAYING WITH THE MARTYRS
Preface by Madeleine L'Engle

PRAYING WITH JOHN DONNE
AND GEORGE HERBERT
Preface by Richard Harries

Books by
David Adam

THE EDGE OF GLORY
Prayers in the Celtic tradition

Modern prayers which recapture the Celtic way of intertwining divine glory with the ordinariness of everyday events.

THE CRY OF THE DEER
Meditations on the Hymn of St Patrick

Meditations leading to practical exercises which take us deeper into the prayer experience in affirming the Presence of God.

TIDES AND SEASONS
Modern prayers in the Celtic tradition

A series of prayers which echo the rhythms of creation, finding their parallels in our spiritual lives and in the highs and lows of all human experience.

THE EYE OF THE EAGLE
Meditations on the hymn 'Be thou my vision'

David Adam takes us through the words of the Celtic hymn, 'Be thou my vision', discovering the spiritual riches that are hidden in all our lives.

POWER LINES
Celtic prayers about work

A series of modern prayers about work which incorporates the insights of the Celtic tradition. The book opens up Celtic patterns of prayer to focus on the work we all do in the presence of God.

BORDER LANDS
The Best of David Adam

An SPCK hardback edition of selections from the first four of David Adam's books—an ideal introduction to Celtic spirituality.

More books from

TRIANGLE

THE VOICE FROM THE CROSS
by Donald Coggan

In a series of striking meditations on Jesus' seven last words from the cross, the former Archbishop of Canterbury challenges us all to look more deeply into the central events of the Christian faith.

SAINTS ALIVE!
Biblical Reflections on the Lives of the Saints
by Michael Marshall

Saints Alive! offers a six-week series of daily meditations providing Bible readings and reflections on the way particular saints have lived out biblical principles and ideas.

THE TRUTH ABOUT LOVE
Re-introducing the Good News
by William Countryman

A remarkably fresh presentation of the message of Jesus, written with a pastoral concern for all Christians. William Countryman challenges us all to find the authentic good news and live abundantly in faith, hope and love.

PATHS OF THE HEART
Prayers of Medieval Christians
edited by John Blakesley
Foreword by Brother Ramon SSF

A collection of moving and inspiring prayers to enrich Christian devotional lives by their imaginative and perceptive spirituality

Triangle and SPCK Books
can be obtained from
all good bookshops.
In case of difficulty, or for a
complete list of all our books, contact:
SPCK Mail Order
36 Steep Hill
Lincoln
LN2 1LU
(tel: 0522 527 486)